More Praise for YOUR LAWYER: AN OWNER'S MANUAL

"A must-read for lawyers who want to know what their clients are really thinking—or should be thinking. A timely and readable guide to achieving maximum client satisfaction with the services lawyers provide."

> —Steven L. Bashwiner, Esq., Katten Muchin Rosenman LLP

"No book has ever offered such helpful advice on the legal problems of family businesses. The chapter on litigation offers uniquely valuable insights for controlling litigation costs and improving the outcome of any case. This chapter alone is far more valuable than the book's price."

> —Harry Seigle, Chairman, Seigle's Inc.

"Good counsel from a wise counselor. Krasnow's thoughts on finding, evaluating, and motivating good lawyers should be read by every business owner who has ever been dissatisfied with his lawer or is thinking of choosing a new lawyer."

> —Paul Levy, chairman, North American Bear Company, Inc., Prairie Management and Development, and East Bank Storage Company

Your Lawyer: An Owner's Manual

A Business Owner's Guide to Managing Your Lawyer

HENRY C. KRASNOW

CHICAGO

Printed in Canada.

Library of Congress Cataloging-in-Publication Data

Krasnow, Henry C.
    Your lawyer: an owner's manual: a business owner's guide to managing your lawyer / Henry C. Krasnow.
       p.   cm.
    Summary: "A guide to helping small business owners and managers to find, work with, and motivate attorneys. Offers an overview of the legal process and how to work though legal problems"—Provided by publisher.
    ISBN-13: 978-1-932841-12-1 (pbk.)
    ISBN-10: 1-932841-12-1 (pbk.)
    1. Attorney and client—United States—Popular works.   2. Small business—Law and legislation—United States—Popular works.
I. Title.
    KF311.K73 2005
    346.73'0652—dc22

2005017909

10 9 8 7 6 5 4 3 2 1

Agate books are available in bulk at discount prices. For more information, go to agatepublishing.com.

TABLE OF CONTENTS

Part I: Dealing With Lawyers

◆ *To my wife Lucile,*
without whose love, help, support, encouragement,
prodding, and advice this never would have been possible.

ACKNOWLEDGEMENTS

This book required nowhere near the effort or creativity of even a minor work of fiction. Yet there are countless people who have contributed, sometimes unknowingly, to its creation.

First, there is my assistant, Carol Mohica who has typed, edited, retyped, reedited, and then finally retyped and reedited again the many drafts of the manuscript that led to this book.

In addition, there are my clients, to whom I will be forever in debt, who taught me everything that I was able to write about. The most notable in this group, and the ones from whom I learned the most, are (in alphabetical order) Anthony J. Augustine, Dennis R. Egidi, Marvin Fohrman, Paul A. Levy, Dan B. Shure, and Jay Tribby. To them, and the many others who not only asked me for my advice and then trusted me enough to act on it, and who also actually paid me for it, I will be forever grateful.

And finally, I want to acknowledge the considerable help and advice given to me by my wife, who tirelessly read all of the drafts and corrected my many mistakes, and my friends John Ward (who persuaded me that my thoughts and perceptions might be interesting to someone other than my family and the young lawyers hired by my firm who had no choice but to listen to me) and Howie Krakow (who made a selfless and valiant effort to make the manuscript more readable).

◆ PART I

Dealing With Lawyers

One

What Is This Book About?

The purpose of this book is to explain how your behavior and your statements—such as how you phrase the questions you ask your lawyer, how you react to the answers, and how you compensate your lawyer—affect the advice your lawyer ends up giving you, and in particular the value of that advice. The key to getting higher-quality services from your lawyer is the same as getting higher-quality services or products from any other vendor—be a better buyer and manager.

Ultimately, you want lawyers to add value to your business. But they need your help. This book will not actually solve any legal problems. But it should go a long way toward helping you save money, and actually make more money, by changing how you understand and address the legal problems facing your business.

Applying the ideas presented in this book can save you time, frustration, and money. They should help you better understand the legal process—what happens, why it happens, why it's often so frustrating, and what you can do to make it work better for you—so that you will make wiser decisions. You will understand what issues you can control and what issues you should not waste time or money trying to control. Ultimately, the more you control the legal process (and the less you try to control the uncontrollable), the more likely you are to be satisfied, both emotionally and financially, with the outcome.

If you are a business owner, this book should help you identify quickly and accurately whether you are working with a good lawyer, find a good lawyer if you wish to, and work with your lawyer to get higher-quality legal services.

Jokes about lawyers always get big laughs on a golf course or at a dinner party. (Shakespeare's suggestion, "First, let's kill all the lawyers," is, of course, funny. But if you are ever sued for a breach of contract, or want to merge your company with another, you will still call a lawyer and not a playwright.) But what many business owners fail to realize is that often those jokes point out *solvable* problems.

Lawyers are driven by their marketplace and their customers' expectations to a far greater degree than even they sometimes realize. Like all vendors, they respond to what they think will make their customer (or client) satisfied with their work. Business owners, as consumers of legal services, will receive the highest quality of products or services from their vendors—even lawyers—when they articulate realistic desires and expectations, and act appropriately and decisively when those desires and expectations are not being met.

A classic example of an unrealistic client that every lawyer has met is the business owner involved in a small dispute who tells his or her lawyer, "I will not settle! I'd rather pay you than pay those liars!"

To the surprise of most business owners, few lawyers are happy to hear what might seem to be a promise of an unlimited budget.

Most lawyers know from bitter experience that this is a client who has unrealistic expectations. Even though most clients may be convinced that they meant what they said at the time they said it, they will undoubtedly change their mind—and then blame their lawyer. When they realize that using a lawyer to fight is more expensive (and much less fun) than they had imagined. Or when they have to spend large amounts of their own time to answer preliminary, or *discovery*, questions, find and produce documents, or testify at a deposition. Or a trial will become imminent and they will realize that they could have compromised for less money than the attorney's fees and they still might lose at the trial.

A lawyer in this position has little incentive to be honest or to give good advice. After all, the client has not asked for or offered to pay for honesty or good advice. Few lawyers have ever had a client like this later say, "I really regret that I didn't listen to you when you told me to compromise, or even ask you what you thought was best." On the contrary, most experienced lawyers have stories about how they were blamed for having billed too much or for not having "made" the judges grant their clients what they wanted.

The single most important thing to understand when dealing with lawyers is that, for better or worse, they are very literal. If you go to a friend or a therapist and say, "I really want to fire my business partner," they will assume that what you mean is, "I really want to tell you how angry I am at my business partner so that I can get it off my chest."

But if you go to your lawyer and say, "I really want to fire my business partner," your lawyer will think that you mean, "I really want to fire my business partner." If you say you want to fight a claim "to the death," and then later question whether the legal work done was "really necessary," your mixed messages will destroy the lawyer's motivation to develop a healthy collaborative relationship.

So: if you want good services from motivated lawyers, you need to be realistic about your goals, you need to be clear in what you say and how you say it, and you need to avoid giving mixed messages. If you tell your lawyer something on one day and then later contradict yourself, with your words or with your actions, your lawyer will be confused about what you really mean or want. As a result you will almost certainly get worse service and frustrating results. And you can be sure that blaming the "system," or not paying your lawyer, will not get you better service or better results.

Some readers of this book may be advisors or consultants to businesses. Many might be consultants who have training in human behavior and are brought in to deal with some of the more complicated emotional problems involved in running businesses. I hope these readers will take from this book a better understanding of the ways lawyers think, the contributions that lawyers can make, and the logic and workings of the legal system.

Some of My Best Friends Are . . .

I want to make my personal bias about lawyers clear—I'm a lawyer and most of my best friends are lawyers. I have the highest respect for many lawyers and did not write this book to criticize, condemn, or insult lawyers or question their intelligence or integrity. On the contrary—I have worked with lawyers and judges who are some of the smartest men and women I have ever met. These are people who have an incredibly wide range of knowledge, emotional sensibility, practical insight, and genuine wisdom. They are clever and creative problem-solvers who operate with the highest level of integrity, honesty, and ethical conduct. I believe most of these lawyers and judges are harder working, more honest, and at least as intelligent, clever, forthright, and dedicated as the people who populate any other profession. (That is not to deny that there are incompetent, dim, and dishonest lawyers. Unfortunately, incompetence and dishonesty seem to exist in every profession and almost every corner of society.)

Similarly, this book is not meant to be a condemnation or criticism of our legal system. This system has been painstakingly created, refined, and adjusted over the last 225 years. Yes, it may be very complicated, time-consuming, and expensive to navigate this system. But we live in a very complicated society. This system may not work perfectly, but neither does anything else. Ultimately, no matter how often or how passionately people may complain about this system, one thing is clear. Complaining about it will not change it. To get better results, you need to stop complaining and work toward understanding it and working within it to get the best results for your businesses.

We Are Highly Trained Professionals, or, Don't Try This at Home

Finally, this book is not meant to make you capable of handling your own legal problems. It is not a do-it-yourself manual. It will not train you to be a lawyer.

A good lawyer (the kind of lawyer described in more detail in chapters two, three, and four) has had many years of training beyond just four years of college and three years of law school. Of course, good lawyers must know a lot of legal rules, but knowing these rules is not nearly enough. In fact, these rules are not secret; they are available to everyone, and many people with good memories can learn them if they are willing to study.

Good lawyers have also had years of experience from which they have learned which of these many different legal rules are going to be applied in which situations, and how people react in those situations when those rules are applied. Good lawyers are very accurate in predicting people's behavior in the different situations likely to occur in the course of solving a specific problem. Good lawyers' judgment is difficult to find, and more difficult to replicate.

Anyone who doubts this might consider the learning curve of someone trying to master chess. It's relatively easy to learn the rules—how the chess pieces move on the board. But you need years of study, reflection, and practice to learn how to develop strategies that take into account the interplay of the rules, the infinite possibilities of what the person sitting on the other side of the board will do, and which of your responses will have the desired effect on the outcome of the game. No one can become a good chess player simply by learning the rules. A client once pointed out to me that he wanted a lawyer "who was not playing checkers when the other side is playing chess."

The work of good lawyers can appear deceptively simple. After all, once they have quickly sorted through all the available options and eliminated the impractical alternatives, their suggestion of the best course of action seems obvious. Nevertheless, the best solution is not obvious. Avoid the temptation to think that you can do it yourself. Certainly, no readers of this book, whether business owners or business advisors, would ever suggest that a lawyer could learn to do *their* work just as well as they do by reading a short book and watching them work. The old saying is almost always true: "A man who acts as his own lawyer has a fool for a client."

▶ *Two*

Why Hire a Lawyer?

Let's be clear about one thing. Unless you commit a crime for which the death penalty is a possibility, you can probably live your life without ever hiring a lawyer. As with the work of plumbers, electricians, or accountants, you can do it yourself or live without their help. Similarly, if you think doctors are too expensive, or scare you, you are perfectly free to ignore your high temperature, your severe headaches, or the strange lump under your skin, and many people do. Some of these conditions will go away without anyone's help.

Ultimately, lawyers are advisors or consultants. If you don't think their advice is worth what they charge, you simply should not ask for that advice. If you don't think you need their advice, or if you think you can't afford their advice, or if you think you can do it just as well without their advice, of if you think you are always telling lawyers what to do and they don't seem to add any value, or if you think you know what to do better than lawyers do, then use your head—don't hire them.

There are only three good reasons to hire others for their services:

- if you believe they have information or skills that you don't;
- if you believe that getting that information and skill is worth the price that you will have to pay;
- or if you believe that they can do something that you'd prefer not to do yourself.

If you ask lawyers about their fees and they seem too high, then hire someone with lower fees, or hire no one at all. In the long run, you always get what you pay for. You may find that by attempting to negotiate a relatively simple business transaction yourself, you will be confronted with a terrain that makes you feel you are walking through a minefield without a map. If you find yourself in this position, hiring someone to guide you through this minefield may then seem a worthwhile expense.

The Canoe at the Waterfall

When should you consult a lawyer? That's hard to say.

Imagine you're planning a canoe trip. Do you need a river guide now? Not really. You've got a book describing the river that shows only one area of potential problems.

Eventually you find yourself in your canoe paddling down the river. You know the general direction you are heading and you have a rough idea of where you want to stop. Do you need a river guide now? Hardly.

But there's a bothersome rumble way off in the distance. It could be traffic—perhaps cars and trucks driving over a busy bridge. It could be thunder. Or it could be the sound from the whitewater that was described in the book you read. Do you need a river guide now? Maybe. It would be nice to know what lies ahead. But say you're the self-sufficient type who hates asking for help and you have friends who bragged that *they* paddled other rivers just like this one without paying for help, and you're certainly smarter and tougher than they are, and, after all, river guides charge by the hour and can be very expensive.

Later, the sound gets louder. Do you need a river guide now? Who knows? It would make you feel better to know how rough the ride is likely to get. But you've been in rough water before, and there was never a problem. Certainly, you don't want to pay a guide if it turns out that you could have solved the problem yourself.

After a few more hours of paddling, the speed of the river has picked up, the shores are rocky, and there do not seem to be any easy points to get off the river and portage the canoe over what is unmistakably approaching whitewater. You're not sure how to get out of the current of the river.

Do you need a river guide now? Yes. Absolutely. But this is a terrible time to try to find one. You need help immediately. You no longer have time to shop for the best guide. You certainly don't have time to shop prices. Even if you could find the best guide, or even a moderately good guide, and even if money were no issue, there may be nothing that anyone can do. Paddling over a waterfall is something that can only be done by cartoon characters or superheroes. There is a point beyond which no river guide—no matter how good, how smart, how strong—can help you.

Good lawyers, like good river guides, have the ability to help you *avoid* trouble. There are circumstances where, if you're already in trouble, it's too late for anyone to help you as much as they could have if you had only consulted them earlier. The damage done by your poor planning is irreversible.

The longer you wait to hire an attorney, the smaller your chances of getting or keeping yourself and your company out of trouble. A good lawyer will alert you to potential problems; explain the consequences of those problems; give you the options that are the most likely to lead to your success; give you time to decide how to proceed; and give you the opportunity to execute the option you choose.

If you look for a lawyer before you have a problem, you can make a better choice. You can determine if you and the attorney seem to be a good match. You can discuss compensation, incentives, and the best possible way to work together. And you can do all of that without any pressure.

This might mean you'll begin paying fees to avoid something that never happens. But saving a relatively small amount of money should not be the focus of your thinking. Almost everyone over the age of fifty has an annual medical checkup, even though many have no symptoms and hope that nothing will be found. When the doctor finds nothing wrong, few people feel they have wasted their time or money.

The basic rule about hiring an attorney is this: the most expensive lawyer, who is also the one who is most limited in what he or she can do, is the one you hire *after* you're in trouble. Many lawyers are consulted by people whose canoe is halfway over the falls. Inevitably, those people spend far too much in legal fees and get too little value in return.

And then—of course—they blame their lawyer.

What Do Lawyers Do?

On television and in movies, lawyers often stand in front of a jury and, using nothing but style, guile, brilliance, eloquence, and intuition, get the villain or the lying witness to admit wrongdoing and thus save their innocent client from an unfair conviction or a devastating loss.

The lawyer provides drama while the script provides justice! After all, what flesh-and-blood mortal could have ever goaded Jack Nicholson, a hardened Marine general, into blurting out, "The truth. You want the truth? Well, you can't handle the truth!"

In real life, justice is much harder to find and a lawyer's role is both much less dramatic and much more complex.

1. Lawyers structure business relationships.

Business relationships can be as emotionally and financially complex as a marriage. Poorly structured business relationships will lead to problems just as certainly as dysfunctional personal relationships.

An example: A company that builds websites was contracted to develop a site for a large firm. There were long, involved discussions about this new site's look, purpose, and functionality. A delivery date was agreed upon, and so was the fee. The web designer was convinced that the best way to show self-confidence in her work was by allowing the customers to pay nothing until the job was done and they were satisfied with the result.

When the website was delivered—on time—the customers didn't like it. Over time, and without realizing it, they had changed their goals for the website, but had not clearly spelled out all these changes to the web designer. They asked for revisions of the final product. The designer realized that the clients had changed their mind, but thought that there was nothing she could do but live by the rule, "The customer is always right." The clients were not aware of their own behavior, but knew they did not have to pay until they were satisfied, and thought the designer had either just not been listening carefully or was not skillful enough. There had been no discussions about extra charges for revisions, and the designer felt obligated to make her clients happy, because if she didn't, she might not get paid any money. So she made the changes.

The client still didn't like the work. *More* changes were made. But the result was still disappointing to them and, as more time passed, they became more angry about the many lost opportunities from not having their website up and running. Eventually they gave up and hired another website designer. The original designer, despite her very hard work, got paid nothing. The original contract didn't call for compensation based on the amount of effort put into the project; there was simply a price to be paid upon delivery of an acceptable website. Since the client didn't accept delivery, they felt they didn't owe anything.

Both the designer and the customer are now angry; after all, both sides feel that they had fulfilled all their promises and been betrayed. They didn't see any fault in their own behavior and thus had no desire to compromise. A lawsuit seems inevitable, even though it will consume a large amount of money and time. The moral and legal issues of who is "right" are not obvious.

Everyone would have benefited from structuring this relationship to avoid the communication problem. In other words, everyone would have been happier if they had taken into account the fact that in the course of a job—especially a creative job—people often change their minds and misunderstandings occur. Advance planning for predictable misunderstandings and disappointments is not negative or impolite. On the contrary—it's simply good business.

The website designer now has a better structure for her business relationships. It is not a complicated written contract. Rather, it is a simple contract that creates a healthier structure for both parties—designer and customer—because it recognizes that no matter how hard someone works, the customer's thinking may evolve, imperiling their satisfaction. She now requires that she and her customers periodically meet to discuss whether her work to date is satisfactory; as each stage is approved, the customer pays for that portion of the work. There is an agreed-upon dollar figure for the design work, for creating the site map, and for delivering a site that's ready to go online. That way, she finds out early if customers change their mind or if she had misunderstood their instructions. Getting the final payment is not an all-or-nothing, high-stakes gamble for both sides. It's just the last in a series of small gambles. It's a better business relationship for both the buyer and the seller because it minimizes the financial consequences of misunderstandings or frustrated expectations.

Because of their experience in working with the consequences of dysfunctional business relationships, good lawyers are very helpful in building business relationships that work. Contrary to what clients may at first think, being a good lawyer is not a matter of drafting an agreement with clever words that benefits one side at the expense of the other. It's much more about defining the parties' specific areas of responsibility so that both sides clearly understand what is being requested, what risks they are taking, and how much it will cost.

Good lawyers have gone through these discussions before. They understand the issues, they know what questions to ask to help the parties reach agreement, they are bold enough to ask direct questions and insist on clear answers, and they can help everyone define a business relationship that has a high likelihood of withstanding the test of time and the pressures created by predictable change. Remember, lawyers are very literal. This means that they will try to get everyone, not just you, to say exactly what they mean and then, ideally, create a written document that will assure that everyone lives up to their promises.

2. Lawyers structure agreements and put them in writing.

"Well," you might think, "why can't I just write the agreement myself? I was an English major and even have a published short story to my credit."

Certainly, you can write your own agreements. But agreements require a breed of clarity that a good lawyer spends a career perfecting and can do much better than an amateur. It may be strange to think of a lawyer as a professional author, but it is true. Many novelists cannot write poetry, just as very few poets can write good contracts. Writing clear, unambiguous contracts that offer sensible business solutions to predictable problems is a skill that not even all lawyers possess. The most typical example of the problems that are created by lay authors is the use of the word "may" as opposed to the use of the word "shall" or "will." Many people avoid using the words "shall" or "will" because they seem too harsh, too demanding, too concrete. Thus, they might write, "You agree that for $200,000 I may become a partner, at which point I can have a veto over decisions to spend more than $50,000." This is dramatically different than saying, "If I pay you $200,000 within six months, I will be a partner with a veto over decisions to spend more than $50,000." Unfortunately, the politeness demonstrated by the use of "may" runs the risk of leading to a very impolite dispute in the future.

In reality, there are very few agreements that *must* be in writing to be enforceable. Except for some limited exceptions, oral agreements are just as "legal" as written agreements. Many successful people still do business the "old-fashioned" way—almost entirely on oral agreements and trust. Many law firms do not have written partnership agreements. The partners trust each other and are often simply too busy writing contracts for their clients to do it for themselves.

That said, it is still usually a very good idea to write down and sign the terms of most agreements. Even if the agreement is between good friends or family members, having it in writing can be very beneficial. As Aaron Pervin, a prominent Canadian business consultant, once wrote, "Just because people are family does not mean they should not put things in writing." Wanting a written agreement is not a display of distrust or disloyalty. Even though there are many business owners who might not believe this, putting an agreement in writing is not suggested by lawyers as a way of boosting their fees by starting a fight.

How does putting it in writing help anyone other than the lawyer?

- The exercise of putting an agreement in writing while it is fresh in each party's mind helps clarify what everybody is, in fact, agreeing to. Imagine Fred, a business owner whose business is faltering. He goes to David, a good friend, who loans him $100,000 to cover payroll. Although the business prospers, it does not have enough cash to easily pay back the loan. Fred and David are playing golf. David asks about being repaid, and Fred says that he would like to delay repaying the loan but that it will continue to accrue interest. David, who is about to tee off, says, "That's okay, I'll just consider it as capital." The company is eventually sold and, although Fred offers to repay David's loan and every penny of interest, David is not satisfied and feels cheated. He thought that by leaving his money in the business and being exposed to risk, he should get a percentage of the sales price. If a good business lawyer had been asked to put this in writing, the contract would have made Fred and David focus on what they really meant, since what they actually said did not have as precise a meaning as each had thought. There is little doubt that the breach in their relationship could have been avoided if either of them had insisted that their agreement be put down as a written contract.
- The process of putting an agreement in writing tends to reveal potential problems that may not have been discussed or even considered. A good contract averts

disputes because it specifies everyone's obligations. Rather than creating tensions, it can make people feel much more comfortable because they now have a clear idea of each person's expectations and responsibilities. Imagine if David and Fred had been more specific and had agreed that in exchange for leaving his money in the business, David would get a "fifteen percent piece of the business"—they would be "partners." Unfortunately, those words also do not have a clear meaning. Did Fred have to limit his salary so that David would get a dividend? As partners, would David have any say in management? Would David ever have the right to get a salary? These, and many more questions, need to be answered in order to define the relationship that David and Fred only began to outline. A good business lawyer would have asked these questions and avoided the almost guaranteed possibility of serious problems if the business had been successful. Ironically, since there was no written contract to resolve the potential problems that would occur if the business were successful, their friendship might last longer if the business were to fail.

- Even well-meaning and honest people forget what was actually said. It is not only possible, but actually normal, for two people to have differing memories of a verbal agreement. That doesn't make them liars or bad people. It just means that they remember things differently. A written contract is a very effective way to avoid the conflict and confusion that can result from the natural process of forgetting.

- Some people are dishonest and are prepared to lie. Sad but true. These people will try to take advantage of a lack of clarity. A written agreement makes doing this more difficult.

- When people die, a written agreement avoids disputes among their heirs. If everything is written down, there is no need to rely on the survivor whom the heirs may not trust to remember the details of the agreement that they feel was unfair to them. Even if David and Fred trust each other like brothers and are able to come to fair resolutions of every imaginable dispute, if David were to die, will his widow or children believe Fred's version of their "deal"?

- Sometimes there is a need to show an agreement to third parties. Banks, insurance companies, other shareholders, or potential suppliers who might be worried about Fred's business's liquidity problems are much more likely to be comfortable if they can see in writing that David's $100,000 is capital, and not a loan that has to be paid back.

- A signed document will almost always influence the way people act in the future. When there is no possibility of misunderstanding the existence and content of an agreement, people will more readily and clearly understand the consequences of their actions. Under these circumstances, they become highly motivated to behave according to the agreement.

An important note: Just because an agreement is written by an attorney doesn't mean that it needs to be written in complicated legal language. In fact, the goal of a good lawyer should always be the opposite. One of the possible uses of a written agreement is to have it interpreted and enforced by a third party (a judge) if there is a dispute. The result of that third party's interpretation will be more accurate and more predictable if the contract is clearly written and easy to understand.

3. Lawyers ask the impolite questions that often need to be asked.

Good lawyers know enough about the future to realize, with assurance, that they usually can't guarantee what it holds. As a result, they will invariably (and sometimes to the chagrin or annoyance of their clients) ask many very important questions that all begin with, "What happens if...?"

What happens if you die? What happens if you sell the business? What happens if you get sick or want to retire? What happens if you run out of money? What happens if you don't perform as promised, even though you have a great track record? What happens if there's a strike and a critical material cannot be obtained? What happens if the government does not approve the project? What happens if the law changes?

The initial discussions between two people who want to do business together are often very circumspect. Everyone wants to be upbeat and positive. No one wants to offend, be negative, doubt the promises of the other people, be thought of as untrusting. This is often a good thing. After all, there is no reason to get into deep analysis of the fine points or "what ifs" until the basics have been agreed upon and each side is convinced that this can be a good deal.

Unfortunately, and all too often, discussions end there. Further conversation addressing the possibility of problems never happens, as everyone basks in the afterglow of having hit upon a win-win plan where all will make money if things go as expected. No one enjoys or appreciates someone who only tries to figure out the ways that something can go wrong. Who needs that kind of negative energy?

Good lawyers know, from years of experience, that the best-laid plans often go awry. Things change. My grandfather used to say, "The way to make God laugh is to make plans." Almost nothing goes exactly as planned. Business is always a struggle. The sad fact is that everyone needs to have someone to talk with who will think of what can go wrong. A good lawyer can help even the most cautious business owner consider the risks in a potential business deal and the likelihood and consequences of those risks occurring.

Many business owners get frustrated by how difficult it can be to answer a good lawyer's questions. But discouraging those questions is a mistake. Lawyers should be encouraged to raise issues about which there was no agreement. They should create scenarios based on likely future events. Lawyers should not make the business decisions—only you can do that. But they should ask the questions that raise the issues that you and the other business owner may not have thought of raising or were simply too polite to mention.

When all of the likely problems are foreseen and discussed, a solution can be agreed upon and responsibly assigned in advance. Trying to find solutions under the pressure created by the prospect of a major loss from an unanticipated development can lead to the sort of finger-pointing that can corrode the relationship. If the solution to a potential problem is not discussed until after it arises, one side often finds that it may have certain fortuitous and unexpected economic leverage, which too often leads to a resolution that no one would have thought of as fair when the deal was in its planning stages. Lawyers help keep business relationships on track by helping to anticipate future problems.

The goal of both business owners and their lawyers should be to agree on sensible plans that specify what will occur if particular future events happen or don't happen. In that way, an agreement can be reached which makes an appropriate course of action clear when problems arise, and places rewards and incentives properly to encourage behavior most likely to lead to a win-win solution—and not an irresolvable dispute.

4. Lawyers predict the future.

By being part psychologist, part economist, and part fortuneteller, a good lawyer should provide valuable predictions of what the future holds. Of course, a lawyer should not be asked to predict the answer to a question concerning marketplace conditions, such as how the price of steel might react to the bankruptcy of a large domestic steel manufacturer. But good lawyers should be able to predict with a higher-than-normal degree of accuracy how a contract will be interpreted, or what will happen if certain promises are broken, or how the other party to a contract will behave if certain disputes occur or if certain expectations are not fulfilled.

They can and should predict what a judge will do if a dispute is presented in certain ways, or what the odds are of a jury making a certain decision.

Experienced lawyers have spent years observing how business-people react in certain business settings. Their sense of what the future holds should help their clients avoid problems, or make contingency plans for dealing with a predictable problem. My friend Jim used to work for a wine distribution company as a com-missioned salesman. He was very good at what he did, and ended up making some connections that got him the beer and wine con-cession for the local major league baseball park. His commissions skyrocketed, and in a few months he was earning more than all the other salesmen and almost as much as the company's owners. The owners were grateful for Jim's success, but saw no reason why they should pay him so much money if they could avoid it. Dur-ing the next year, the owners made it a point to get to know the people at the ballpark who did the purchasing, and as soon as they could, they made the ballpark a "house account." This meant Jim no longer got commissions on the revenue from the sales he had originated. The owners, aware of Jim's skills as a salesman, offered him a new territory that would allow him to earn more than the other salesmen, but far less than he had made with the ballpark as his account. Feeling, for good reason, that he had been stabbed in the back, Jim quit his job.

Although Jim had a problem that a lawyer probably could not have solved, a good lawyer would have seen it coming. After all, the company's owners would predictably not want a salesman who earned as much as they did, especially when they could replace him for a fraction of his cost. By realizing that he was exposed to the risk of losing his account, my friend might have had the time and opportunity to strike a deal with the company owners before they had solidified the new relationship with the ballpark. He might have gotten them to agree to give him a permanent commission even if the ballpark became a house account. He might have had economic leverage because of his ability to move the account to a competitor. Or, the advance knowledge of what would probably happen might have encouraged him to begin looking for a job before the inevitable occurred.

5. Lawyers resolve disputes.

Business plans, like most everything else in life, are imperfect. Inevitably, something will go wrong.

Although many people believe that lawyers make money by purposefully causing fights and then making them worse, the truth is that when there are disputes or disagreements, good lawyers can, and usually do, help resolve them.

One of the first things good lawyers can do is define a dispute. First they can provide a clear analysis of the situation. Then, they help analyze the problem from two different perspectives—who is "legally" right and most likely to prevail in court, and who has the economic power to force a resolution. These are questions that often have dramatically different answers.

Imagine a business that has hired a contractor to build its new factory. In the middle of the job, the contractor—not trusting the owner to be fair once the work is completed and worrying that the owner may not have enough money to pay for the whole job—insists on immediate payment for "extra" work. The owner feels this work should be covered by the original bid price. The architect thinks that the owner is right, but can't guarantee that a judge would agree if there were a lawsuit. The contractor refuses to continue the work without agreement on this charge. The owner, feeling that he is being "held up" and taken advantage of (which, by the way, he is), refuses to pay the disputed amount and begins taking bids from new contractors to finish the work. These people are playing very high-stakes poker in which only a new contractor is guaranteed to win. A new contractor will charge a premium to finish the work of someone else under emergency circumstances. The owner still runs the risk of having to pay the first contractor its lost profit if a judge determines that he was wrongfully fired. Ultimately, it may be worth paying the unearned "extra" charge to complete the job and avoid the risk of a major loss or delay. The owner may have been "right," but the contractor still has considerable economic leverage.

A lawyer should help by suggesting ways to lower the stakes. An easy solution for everyone might be to agree that the disputed amount be put up by the owner and held in escrow by a neutral party. That way, the issue of the disputed extra charge can be decided by itself after the work is done and the tempers have cooled. And the contractor's concern about the owner's financial condition should go away.

When working at their best, lawyers facilitate rational discussion. People are often angry during disputes, but lawyers can help encourage an unemotional exchange of information that helps reach sensible compromises.

Also, most people do not do well in situations that involve conflict. It upsets them. It frustrates them. It makes them nervous and incapable of acting or thinking rationally. But lawyers deal with conflict for a living. It's what they do. And it's why they can be so good at resolving disputes. But sometimes the dispute simply cannot be resolved. One of the biggest services that lawyers perform is to help their clients' face uncomfortable situations without unjustified fear that can get in the way of reaching a fair resolution. Many businesspeople pride themselves on being good negotiators. But even they can benefit from an attorney's advice during the negotiating process. You can't have a good cop/bad cop situation unless there are two cops.

Of course, sometimes the best thing a lawyer can do is to provide people and businesses with access to the courts. That's important, and sometimes it's the best solution to a problem. Courts exist to resolve disputes. Not all lawsuits take years, and knowing when litigation can quickly solve a problem is of great value.

Imagine three people who set up a partnership that requires the agreement of all three for the partnership to act. They sign a contract to sell a building, and when the closing comes near, one partner refuses to sign the deed, hoping to use this as leverage to get the other two partners to pay her money she would otherwise not get. The buyer is threatening a lawsuit for the hundred thousand dollars it spent on its due diligence, loan fees, survey, title costs, and attorneys' fees. It can be a relatively simple matter for the lawyer for the two "good" partners to get a judge to enter an order, on an emergency basis, requiring the reluctant partner to sign the deed that she had agreed to deliver months earlier when she had signed the contract to sell.

As a general rule, many people prefer to avoid conflict at any cost. When you do get involved in a business dispute, it's important for you to realize that it is very unlikely that you will get everything you want. Even if you win in court, you almost never get back your attorneys' fees. When you hire a good lawyer, you're hiring someone whose *only* goal is to help you get the best possible resolution. But that does not mean you will always "win." No lawyer—even the most expensive or skillful lawyer—is likely to get you everything you want. You need to have a much more realistic goal. At best, a good lawyer can help you resolve the disputes efficiently—that means without taking undue risk, while giving due regard to the strengths and weaknesses of your position.

6. Lawyers help minimize taxes.

You are undoubtedly familiar with the lethal combination of terms, "tax law."

Tax law can be frightening. And if you don't know what you're doing, it can cost you a lot of money.

On the other hand, a good lawyer can save you a lot of money.

An example: In real estate, there is something known as a *1031 exchange*. If you sell a piece of property and make a profit, you normally have to pay taxes. That's understandable.

Often when people sell property, they want to reinvest the profits into another piece of real estate. If that happens, under certain very specific conditions, they can avoid paying taxes. That's what a 1031 exchange is about.

Here's how it works. If you sell a piece of property and use the proceeds to buy a more expensive piece of property, you might avoid all taxes—no matter how much profit you make on the sale—until you make a sale that does not reinvest the proceeds into comparable real estate. That's a very simplistic explanation of the 1031 exchange but, in general, it's pretty accurate. Selling and buying property this way requires extra effort and expense, and it's certainly a bit more complicated. But depending on the profit from the original sale, the tax savings can be enormous.

Any good business attorney can explain the 1031 exchange. But without an attorney, you might not know about it. And if you don't, you could end up paying taxes that could have been avoided.

Tax law is complicated. It requires knowledge, experience, and an ability to pay close attention to the continually changing tax laws. A knowledgeable business attorney can explain the benefits and risks of various ways of setting up and running your business (many of which you might not learn about any other way). This helps you evaluate those choices and provide the structure to put the most beneficial tax saving plans into practice.

7. Lawyers help implement change caused by death, retirement, expansion, or contraction.

Change is inevitable. But as things change, good lawyers should help with some of the adjustments that are necessary. Certainly, your lawyer cannot assuage the uncomfortable feelings that may arise from one brother being chosen over another to be president or chairman of the family business. However, lawyers can help draft new agreements that revise the family's ownership interests and veto powers, define the terms of someone's employment, define obligations and expectations to help avoid future conflict as a business continues to grow and generate profits, or deal with the role of an owner's widow if she becomes the majority stockholder upon inheriting her husband's stock.

All of us know people who actually don't think they will ever die. In fact, that may describe the majority of us. If two people such as that start a business, two people who really think they will never die, neither is likely to consider how to deal with the partner's widow if the partner dies first. A good lawyer can draft documents that make this an easier transition.

8. Lawyers help avoid problems with the government.

Simply keeping a business profitable is a hard enough job for most people. Conforming to the many and varied governmental regulations can make running a profitable business seem impossible.

Your job is to make the right business decisions. Your lawyer can relieve you of a huge burden by being responsible for knowing the governmental rules that apply to your business and helping you comply with them. For most lawyers, it is a simple matter to make sure your corporation's minutes are kept up to date, your annual governmental reports are filed on time, and you are appropriately registered to do business in all the necessary states.

9. Lawyers answer questions and provide a good sounding board.

It is lonely at the top. Many successful business owners have no peers with whom to discuss problems and test possible solutions. And, with the sometimes overwhelming demands of business and family, it's often hard to develop or even remember new ideas. You can't possibly know too much. That's why trusted advisors are always helpful. And your lawyer should be one of the advisors you trust most.

You should have a lawyer with whom you feel free to push for creative solutions—not just explanations to legal questions, but also recommendations and analysis. You don't have to accept your lawyer's advice (and, in fact, a lawyer's advice on business matters may be short on practical wisdom), but the more you discuss critical issues with trusted advisors, the more assurance you'll have that the decisions you make have been well thought through and are wise.

▶ *Three*

The Discovery, Care, and Feeding of a Good Lawyer

A friend once said, "There are two kinds of vacations: good vacations and great vacations." Some business owners might suggest that there are only two kinds of lawyers: expensive lawyers and more expensive lawyers.

Regardless of people's complaints about the cost, temperament, attitude, or wisdom of lawyers, most business owners continue to find lawyers essential. Or as another friend once put it, "Lawyers—can't live with them, can't kill them."

Everyone who owns a business or consults with the owner of a business should cultivate the ability to recognize the difference between good and not-so-good lawyers. All business owners should strive to:

- spot good lawyers when they see them;
- appreciate when they are being given good advice;
- define the lawyer's role in a way that allows lawyers to do what they do best;
- react rationally to a lawyer's advice, especially when it's good advice;
- recognize when something other than good advice is being given.

Accomplishing these goals requires an understanding of the various types of lawyers, the various mistakes that business owners commonly make with lawyers, and the earmarks of good and bad advice.

The Two Kinds of Clients

Before choosing or evaluating a lawyer, a business owner should understand that there are essentially two types of clients:

1. Those who pay a lawyer out of money that they would otherwise take home. These are the typical family or entrepreneurial business owners. People in this position have two notable traits:

   - First, they have no fear of being fired because of a lawyer's mistake. After all, they usually own the company.
   - Second, they are aware that the money they spend on lawyers is money that they could otherwise use for themselves or invest elsewhere in the business—e.g., use it for advertising or a new machine, pay it to themselves or their children, or even give it as a gift to their grandchildren.

   When people pay a $50,000 legal fee, they feel that they have given their lawyer enough money to buy a brand-new Mercedes. The lawyer may not see it this way; after all, the lawyer may take home only a small portion of this money, the rest being eaten up by over-head of 50 percent or more and a share taken by their partners. But from the point of view of the business owner who signed the check, they have still paid the value of a new Mercedes and appropriately expect to receive in return from the lawyer something of equal value.

   Clients like this ask, "What did I get from this lawyer that was worth the new Mercedes I could have bought if I had not paid this money?"

Some lawyers might answer this question by saying, "You got my time paying attention to your matter." For clients like this, that is rarely an adequate answer. A lawyer's time by itself may have value to the lawyer, but it has no value to a business owner.

If you are this kind of client, you should be looking for a lawyer who can answer this question in terms of the value of the advice given or the work done. Lawyers who cannot explain *how or why* their time was valuable to the client will rarely be able to please clients with this mindset.

2. Those who pay a lawyer out of a company's shareholders' money. These people also have two notable traits:

   • First and foremost, they fear being fired if there is a bad result. In other words, if they are put in a position to make a decision based on a lawyer's advice and that decision turns out badly, there is a very significant downside.
   • Second, if the problem gets solved and their company makes or saves a lot of money, the vast majority of that money probably goes into the hands of their boss or the shareholders. And if the lawyer is efficient and costs little money, they may get a gold star, they may get a pat on the head from their boss, or they may even get a slightly larger bonus, but they almost never get to take home the money that the company saved. After all, how many people do you think have received a promotion or the profits generated by spending the legal budget frugally? In other words, if they take a risk, these people have little upside and a large downside.

When choosing a lawyer, you should know which of these categories you fall into. Although everyone knows that business involves risks, entrepreneurial clients make their living evaluating those risks and determining whether the potential reward is worth that risk. They rarely delegate this decision to others. The buck stops in their office. They know that no one can protect them from risk. On the contrary, they prosper in business because they are better than their competitors in managing change and reducing the risk that is inherent in that change.

People who fit this profile should try to work with a lawyer who also understands that business requires the taking of risks and who can evaluate risky alternatives in terms of possible rewards and likelihood of various outcomes. These are often the lawyers who can explain why their services are valuable to the business.

On the other hand, clients who are spending their shareholders' money are often professional managers who, appropriately, have an entirely different agenda. They don't make the major strategic decisions regarding risk—those are made by their companies' senior executives. The major risk that the managers face is losing their job. They are less interested than their entrepreneurial colleagues in a lawyer who will evaluate the risk of various alternatives and then let them decide which risk to take. Their instinctive desire is to reduce the risk of the one thing that is most important to them—losing their job. They want lawyers who will reduce *that* risk—such as "brand-name lawyers" whose advice the boss can never criticize because of the renown of their law firm or the size of their bills. If something goes wrong, these managers want to be able to say to their bosses, "How can you blame me? No one is better than the mega-firm we hired. After all, they have over a thousand lawyers and offices in all major cities. And look how much they charged us." Managers like this might want lawyers who recommend the path that involves the least risk, even if it means forgoing an opportunity that has the chance of a large reward for the company.

For example, imagine a small but profitable company with about thirty people in the central administrative office, one of whom, a sixty-year-old man, has been underperforming. He is chronically late to work in the morning, forgetful, takes breaks that are almost always five or ten minutes too long, and is often grumpy.

If nothing is done, it is only a matter of time until the others in his department start coming in late and extending their breaks. The culture of being on time and giving 110 percent is being gradually eroded. He has been talked to several times, but even though he has apologized and promised to do better, his behavior has not changed. There is no doubt that he must be fired, and the longer this is put off, the harder it will be to repair the damage to the culture of the office.

However, the person who runs the human relations department knows that the company has not kept records of the verbal warnings or of the days or times of the extra-long breaks. Thus, there is no "hard" proof of warnings, the late arrivals or the too-long breaks. The company fears that firing this man will be the beginning of a very bothersome, time-consuming, and expensive age-discrimination case.

Wisely, two lawyers are consulted.

One lawyer gets the facts and says:

> *Of course, if you fire him you will probably be sued for age discrimination. But that might be the lesser of two evils. After all, by keeping him your business risks losing more money as a result of having its culture of hard work destroyed. And if he really is as forgetful as you say, it's only a matter of time until he makes a mistake that will be even more costly. Of course, he may sue you. But he probably knows he's screwing up and may not want to risk the humiliation of a trial where his competence is the issue. If he sues, you can most likely settle for less than the cost of keeping him on. It's your decision, but if it were my company, I'd get him out before his presence totally destroys the culture that took you so much time to develop and which is so valuable.*

The second lawyer, who is equally talented, experienced, and successful, advises:

If you fire him, you may be sued for age discrimination, and your risk of losing that lawsuit is greater because you don't have written evidence of timing all employees and keeping track of when all employees show up to work. You also don't have a personnel file that has a written history of warnings. The safest thing to do to avoid the risk of being sued is to adopt a written policy of timing all employee breaks, keeping a written record of when they arrive, circulating a rule about how many times you can be late, giving written warnings. After about twelve months, you should be able to carefully document all his shortcomings. If you fire him then, you will have a much better defense if he sues. I know that this is expensive and will annoy the other employees, but it's probably just a matter of time until you have to institute these policies and you might as well bite the bullet and do it now. If you don't, the employee's chance of succeeding in his lawsuit is greatly increased. As it is, if you fire him and he sues you, winning the case will be far from a sure thing.

Both lawyers have given "good" advice. But only a business owner is likely to accept the advice of the first lawyer. The head of the human relations department of a company that is owned by others may feel that the second lawyer's advice is "safer."

When interviewing a prospective lawyer, even if it's done casually at a dinner party, business owners should understand what kind of lawyer they want and how the particular lawyer sitting in front of them views the role.

Lawyers who have been trained to identify risk and take any measures possible to reduce it (regardless of the lost potential reward or the cost) rarely work well with entrepreneurial business owners. Businesses face an almost infinite number of risks, but some are no more likely to occur than the sun rising in the west. Someone who works for the largest electrical utility company in the state may want her contracts to cover every possible contingency, no matter how remote, if she thinks that a breach of this contract could create the risk of her losing her job. Few family business owners, on the other hand, would see the point of risking a potentially lucrative business opportunity by prolonging potentially hostile contract negotiations over possibilities that have only a remote chance of occurring. Lawyers who think of creative or new ways to solve problems and who try to evaluate risks in realistic ways often go unappreciated by executives whose jobs would be jeopardized by a bad outcome, no matter how unlikely.

The Three Kinds of Lawyers

There are essentially three types of roles for lawyers:

- *The surrogate parent or older sibling.* Some lawyers understand their role to be like the mother, father, big brother, or big sister their clients never had: someone who will protect them from risk or who will make life fair and safe for them. Lawyers like this will often proudly tell stories of how they rescued their other clients from making serious mistakes—stories that include the phrase, "I would never let a client of mine...." These lawyers often have very happy clients. After all, feeling that your lawyer will protect you in this way can be very comforting.

  However, business owners often tire of this type of lawyer because they soon come to grips with the reality that no one can protect them from risk. They know that if they really wanted to be protected from risk, they would have sold their business long ago and gone to work for the only truly safe and secure employer—the government. Owning a business is, by definition, to be exposed to risk. For business owners, success is normally determined by how well their advisors evaluate risk and recognize opportunities to minimize it, not by how well they avoid it.
- *The gladiator/gunfighter.* Some lawyers view their job as going out to do battle for their clients. Just like gun-

fighters in the Old West, they fearlessly saunter into a dispute or negotiation, brag about their skills, say insulting things about the other disputants and their lawyers, and stand ready to fight it out at high noon. This image is popularized by television and has an undeniably romantic appeal. Lawyers like this often assure their clients, "We won't let anyone take advantage of you that way!" When hearing this, who wouldn't welcome the presence at their side of a "tough" lawyer who will "fight" for their rights? It's exciting. It's dramatic. It's reassuring. It's good theater!

However, the fallacy of this model is that when real gunfighters fought, one was actually wounded or killed. It was their own blood that was spilled. With lawyers, however, only the client's blood (in the form of money or business opportunity) is at stake. Gunfighter wannabes learn early in their careers, "You win some, you lose some, but you get paid for all of them."

If you want theater, this is the lawyer for you. But if you want help with making a rational, cost-effective risk/benefit analysis or dispute resolution, a gunslinger-type may not be your best choice.

- *The consultant.* Some lawyers view themselves as consultants who help the business owner make money by giving honest, rational advice regarding risks, rewards, costs, and alternatives. These lawyers do not perceive their job as standing in the way of rational compromise, or as putting on a show, or as merely focusing on winning without offering an honest assessment of the possibility and consequences of losing, or as fighting to the last penny of their client's bank account. On the contrary—they view their purpose as adding value to the business by helping the owners achieve their goals, or by advising against wasting time trying to achieve the unachievable.

My father once told me a story that I often recall. It was about a young lawyer who was waiting in a courtroom before his first criminal trial. He was very nervous, as losing could mean jail time for his client. Before court started, he was pacing anxiously back and forth in the courtroom. An older friend from law school walked in and started a conversation. When told why the younger man was nervous, the older friend said, "Calm down. Turn around, and tell me what you see." The young lawyer turned to the back of the courtroom and said, "I see the back door of the courtroom." The older friend smiled and said, "Just remember, no matter what happens today, *you* will walk out that door."

The point of the story is that ultimately, no matter how your lawyers act, they will walk out that door. Never forget that it is *your* money and *your* business at stake. You—not your lawyer—should make the decisions from among your alternatives, and your decisions should not be colored by your lawyer's bravado, ego, insecurity, fear of being blamed, or drama. Rather, your decisions should be aided and informed by your lawyer's honest advice and rational analysis.

Being tough or nasty or vicious may sometimes be an appropriate strategy, and it always creates good drama in movies and television, but it should never be a goal. You can be rational and hardheaded while remaining polite and gracious. "Generous" and "gracious" are not the same. Your goal should be financial success, and that can almost always be best achieved by consulting with a lawyer who is smart, resolute, intellectually honest, emotionally mature and focused.

What Are Lawyers' Motivations?

Almost all business lawyers understand that their principal business assets are the relationships with their clients. Yes, their skill and intelligence are important, but without their clients, they usually have few alternatives to make money.

Even though many clients suspect otherwise, lawyers normally view short-term monetary gain as secondary to preserving those relationships. There are exceptions—some divorce lawyers, criminal lawyers, and lawyers who handle injury cases feel that they will most likely only see a client once, and thus they may not put the same value on a long-term relationship. Some may, therefore, try to make as much money on each matter as they can. But most good business lawyers take a more long-term view.

Unfortunately, the lawyer's concern about harming the relationship, or being blamed for a bad result, may subtly motivate the lawyer to hold back the sort of candid advice that is ultimately best for the client. What some might view as conservative advice usually exposes the lawyer to the smallest risk of being blamed. Lawyers, just like almost everyone else in a service business, make money from repeat clients. The easiest sales to make are to happy clients. Finding new clients is much harder than getting repeat business from past clients. Thus, some lawyers inadvertently become concerned only with what can go wrong and forget to consider what can go right.

It is very easy to find a lawyer who will always tell you that you are right. After all, what better way to solidify a relationship than by telling the people who can fire you how smart they are?

Similarly, it is easy to find a lawyer who will almost always help you avoid risks. After all, no risk to the client means no possibility of being blamed.

But anyone who has been in business knows that it is impossible to avoid taking risks. It is crucial to find a lawyer with whom you can have open discussions of your business goals, and who will then honestly—and without fear of being blamed—help you evaluate the potential risks and rewards of any legal decisions. The only lawyers who can do this are those who do not let their advice be colored by a fear of being blamed for a disappointing result that had nothing to do with how well they did their job.

Pick the Right Qualities

The first thing many people negotiate with lawyers is the price. Yes, $300 or more per hour may seem expensive, but how much do we pay dentists or physicians? Seventy-five dollars for a ten-minute office visit is $450 per hour. But even if the lawyer's rate is high, how much of your total budget goes to legal fees? Two percent? Four percent? Higher-priced lawyers are not always better, but make sure that if you lower that percentage by finding a lawyer who is 25 percent cheaper, you don't end up getting mediocre advice.

If you forgo trying to pocket all or part of the relatively small savings that can result from making low fees your first priority, you can work toward increasing your bottom line by finding "value-added lawyering."

Many business owners are probably thinking, "Value-added lawyering? Sounds like an oxymoron, like military intelligence or good airline food."

So, how do you know when lawyers add value? They do the following:

They Provide Risk Analysis

A good lawyer does more than simply return your calls the same day or identify potential risks. A good lawyer will also help you determine the likelihood of that risk occurring. For example, if you are leasing space in a newly built shopping mall, there is always a theoretical risk that the city might take your store through condemnation proceedings. However, this risk is usually very small, and you should want a lawyer who knows that. Once the likelihood of that risk is understood, you and your lawyer can develop a strategy that might, for instance, involve agreeing to the landlord's outrageously unfair lease provision about how to divide the condemnation proceeds in exchange for a more favorable distribution of insurance proceeds if there is a fire. If you're negotiating a contract, wasting time or good will in "winning" issues that may be very unlikely to occur isn't very wise. Even worse, it risks losing the deal entirely.

They Appreciate the Value of Other Experts

Sales, marketing, or public relations experts can often solve problems more effectively than a lawyer. Here's an example: a toy manufacturer

I represented was selling a product named for a parody of a real celebrity's name. The celebrity sued for violation of his rights and sought to prevent further use of his name in the marketing of this product. My legal analysis was that although this was not a clear area of the law, if there were a trial the toy company had better than a 50/50 chance of winning. In other words, I thought my client had the right to do exactly as it was doing.

However, this product was not generating much revenue. Considering this, it did not seem wise to spend a lot of money on attorneys' fees. Yet it also seemed legally unnecessary to throw away the remaining inventory of the product. I suggested that instead of spending tens of thousands of dollars to be "right" in court, my client should discuss with its marketing department the possibility of doing a joint promotion with the celebrity that involved giving away the toys in a public setting. We contacted the celebrity's lawyers and offered to withdraw the product from the market if their client would do the joint press promotion, where the remaining inventory of the product would be passed out at a children's hospital. The event was a huge success—the children were happy, the celebrity was happy, the press was happy, and the publicity was worth more than what could have been made from selling what remained of the product.

The truth is that not all legal problems are best solved with legal solutions. Lawyers can present alternatives that may reduce legal risks. But reducing legal risk is only one part of the enormous and complex puzzle that is business. Remember the inadequate sixty-year-old employee that the company wanted to fire? An outplacement company that could find him a good new job would trump the best records in the hands of the best employment lawyer in the world defending against an age discrimination case before an unpredictable jury.

Quite often, business projects require that lawyers work with other professionals, such as accountants, investment bankers, mortgage bankers, commercial bankers, insurance professionals, and underwriters. On occasion, lawyers are asked to work with management consultants, industrial psychologists, or family business advisors. Too often, lawyers, because of their strong personalities, end up being assigned (or usurping) the leadership of such groups. You—the business owner—need to make sure that any lawyers you put in this kind of position will not undervalue the contributions of those with other skills, or fail to understand they can learn from other highly trained professionals.

They Consider Nontraditional Solutions

At a recent dinner party I sat next to a retired senior partner from a prominent Chicago firm. As is common for older lawyers, we discussed the bad habits of younger lawyers. He then told me the story of how, when he'd been a young lawyer fifty years ago, one of his first assignments from a senior partner was to collect a debt for a client. He considered the obvious alternatives: making a nasty call, writing a threatening letter, or just filing a lawsuit. He then noticed that the guy who owed the money had his office in the same building. So he got up, took an elevator to the debtor's office, and, unannounced, asked to talk with him. They had a nice chat where the lawyer merely asked about why the debt wasn't being paid. No threats, no nasty words, just a straightforward question from one adult to another. The result is that he left with a check for the whole amount. The traditional alternatives probably would have resulted in insults or hurt feelings, which often cause lots of wasted time, postage, paper, and money spent on legal fees.

Good lawyers should be able to look for nontraditional solutions in order to minimize delay and improve communication. They should be encouraged to give you alternative strategies to resolve your problems—and not continually try to please or impress you by engaging in legal activity that, while traditional, is predictably ineffective.

Your goal should be to make sure that your lawyer knows that you appreciate a nontraditional approach more than a confrontation. You need to teach your lawyer that you view "good" legal advice as advice that helps you make money, not advice that helps you spend legal fees for meaningless moral victories in correcting perceived wrongs.

They Understand the Value of Diplomacy and Tact

Years ago, a friend invited me to attend a seminar run by the staff of the vice president of the United States to train volunteers to do advance work for his anticipated campaign for president. At the end of the session, the vice president spoke. He thanked us for volunteering and said:

> *In politics, making enemies is inevitable. But I have tried to make as few enemies as possible and to choose my enemies very carefully. That means I do everything I can to make sure that other people do not make enemies for me without my consent. When you do advance work, you will be representing me—the vice president of the United States, and local dignitaries and office-holders will treat you with great deference and respect. Do not get carried away with your power. I, not you, am the vice president of the United States. Do not forget that reality and do not make an enemy for me without my permission.*

Similarly, business owners may inevitably be forced by some circumstances to make enemies. But wise business owners should insist that they, not their lawyers, choose who their enemies will be. Lawyers should not make enemies without their client's permission. Unfortunately, some clients encourage their lawyers to engage in scorched-earth tactics that do unnecessary harm by offending others for little purpose beyond saber-rattling.

They Understand the Value of Doing Nothing

Sometimes, the best action to take is no action—as a college professor friend has often reminded me, "Doing nothing *is* doing something." As strange and counterintuitive as it may seem, many problems actually go away if they are simply ignored long enough.

On many occasions, playing the waiting game is a very effective tactic. Offering no response—especially when one is expected, hoped for, demanded, or just anticipated—can be a tactic that is very difficult to deal with. Most successful business owners achieved their success by being men or women of action. When someone says something with which they disagree, they have found success by immediately voicing their disagreement.

Yet silence is a strong statement. The effective use of silence is often more powerful than shouting. Clients often call their lawyer about suppliers who, after having delivered an inadequate product, still demand full payment. The client has usually gotten a few angry, threatening, and sometimes insulting letters from the supplier or its lawyer. The wrongful accusations are beginning to raise the emotional heat. Invariably, these business owners want their lawyer to do something to stop the demands, like to write a letter refuting each incorrect claim and showing disdain for the threats. My usual advice—although I am always aware of the risk of my client thinking I'm not tough enough—is that if you just ignore the bills, the letters, and the insults, they may simply go away. To respond in kind by being equally insulting merely raises the stakes of someone doing something that is motivated by anger and not by reason. Silence is a way of saying no, and because it does not involve insults, silence often allows people to make the decision to drop the issue without a fight.

They Look Over the Horizon

Perfect solutions almost never exist. Every solution has the risk of somehow creating another new problem. A good attorney has the ability to look beyond the immediate situation and foresee whether the ripple effect of a proposed solution will cause new problems. It's a rare skill, but an invaluable one.

Years ago, my friend Ed made a mistake that could have been avoided had he consulted a lawyer with this skill. Ed, who owned 100 percent of his company, had a very hardworking, loyal, and valuable employee who said that he wanted to someday own his own company and was talking about leaving. After many long heart-to-heart discussions, Ed realized that he could only keep this person if he were to make him an "owner." Certainly, the valued employee had earned the ten-percent share that Ed wanted to give him, and Ed knew that this employee understood that ownership did not guarantee cash flow; he would not cause trouble as a minority shareholder. Also, Ed knew that as a ten-percent shareholder, his employee could still be fired, and certainly could not outvote Ed on any important corporate governance issues.

The situation worked very well: the employee became even more dedicated and hard working. However, when a fast-growing cancer prematurely took his life, the employee's widow became the owner of the stock and desperately wanted to turn it into cash. Her views were not tempered by any knowledge of the business; on the contrary, she only knew what her husband had told her about how valuable the stock would be someday. Eventually, Ed bought out the widow's stock for more than he thought it was worth, this being the only way to avoid the risk of spending the legal fees necessary to have a trial on the widow's lawsuit claiming minority shareholder abuse.

Seeing over the horizon could have meant negotiating a stockholder agreement with the trusted employee that would have covered the contingencies should either of the stockholders die prematurely. Ed could then have put in writing a formula for repurchasing the stock, as well as for determining all of the other benefits of ownership. And the employee's widow would not have had to experience the anxiety and uncertainty of not knowing what her stock was worth. No one would ever know, but it may be that after considering what the widow's anxiety, uncertainty, and legal expenses, she would have been happier had a lower price been agreed to by her husband before his death.

They Must Understand Economics

The principles of economics can be learned both in schools and through real-life experiences. But regardless of how they are learned, they are extremely helpful when it comes to predicting how other business owners will behave. Sometimes you'll gain favorable contract provisions not because of the skill of your lawyers, but because the other party can't walk away because of economic realities.

Unfortunately, not all lawyers understand these economic principles. But, in order to be truly valuable, a business lawyer should, first and foremost, understand business. A lawyer with broad experience working with many businesses can often add value by bringing new insights to his or her client that a "specialist" is never exposed to.

They Can and Will Educate Your Staff

There are many routine matters that do not need to be handled by a law office. Even junior level lawyers and paralegals can be expensive. Most of them often cost well over $100 per hour.

With some training, your staff can handle many of the tasks that are done by your lawyer's staff. A smart business owner should look for opportunities to identify tasks that the lawyer can train the business' staff to perform. For example, many real estate developers have staff that can do just as good a job as their lawyer's office staff in ordering and negotiating prices for title insurance and surveys. A lawyer who can communicate clearly can train the staff of a sales-oriented manufacturing company to avoid the pitfalls of making contracts that cannot be fulfilled in the course of trying to make a difficult sale.

They Understand the Need for Urgency

Your lawyer knows that not every call from every client is an emergency. But when urgency is required, you want to know that your lawyer understands the importance of the situation and will respond quickly.

A good lawyer who does leasing should know that even though getting the lease signed quickly is hardly an "emergency," each day of delay in having a lease signed costs the shopping center owner money. A few days of delay on each lease decreases the chances of the owner getting an extra month's rent from a new tenant. Even on a small lease for $6,000 per month, a day of delay costs the owner $200. If each year the lawyer delays only ten days on ten leases of this size, the owner will have lost $20,000 of rental income.

If your lawyer's delay is costing you money, there is a simple solution. Don't tolerate it. Either get better service or find a new lawyer.

If You Are Not Part of the Solution, You Will Be Part of the Problem

Although it is rarely helpful to blame the victim, here's the painful truth: the problem with many lawyers is not their lack of skill, nor their lack of talent, nor their lack of integrity, nor their lack of tenacity. It's the fact that their clients do not clearly communicate their goals, or they do not set realistic goals, or they do not listen when they're told their goals are not realistic.

Without realizing it, some business owners regularly encourage their lawyers to act in self-defeating ways. Here are just a few of the things business owners might say that could cause this kind of problem.

1. "You call this being tough?"

Restraint is often one of the least appreciated of a lawyer's skills. Too many business owners are impressed by lawyers who talk tough, who tell stories about how they intimidated others, who constantly talk about how they are not "afraid to fight."

In reality, compromises can save tens of thousands of dollars in legal fees and can often avoid the risk of a bad result. The dollars that you *didn't* pay to a lawyer to keep a dispute going can be invested in marketing, sales, advertising, product development, or factory improvements that will generate far more money than the amount that was lost as a result of the compromise. Years ago, a client asked me to file a lawsuit for $125,000 (which at that time was still considered a very large amount of money). Shortly after I filed the lawsuit, he was offered $70,000 to settle. While he was figuring out whether to take this offer, he asked me the likelihood of his winning the lawsuit. I told him that he had a 75 percent chance of winning all $125,000. Nevertheless, I tried to urge him—gently—to take the money. I reminded him that a trial would not occur for at least another year and that much can happen in that time to the company that owed him the money.

Well, this client got slightly mad at me, and told me that he was disappointed that I wasn't as tough as he would have liked. He decided that he wanted to be tough, and that meant that he would hold out for at least $100,000. After only eleven months, the case was getting close to trial. However, the debtor then went bankrupt and my client got nothing.

Was my client really "tougher" than I was? Although there is no debate that being smart, cunning, rational, and realistic are good qualities in both lawyers and clients, it may not always be in your best interest to criticize lawyers for not being tough enough, since that will inevitably encourage them to ignorer obvious risks for the sake of theater.

2. "All you did was make a few phone calls."

For many people it may be hard to believe that sometimes lawyers can solve problems very quickly and in ways that don't require a lot of intense legal discussions or complicated documents. When that happens, some business owners will do exactly the opposite of what is in their best interest. Instead of praising the lawyer, they question the attorney's bill. After all, they reason, it must have been a simple problem because it was so easily solved. That's precisely the wrong response. Lawyers who have the uncommon wisdom to know that a polite diplomatic phone call can resolve a dispute and avoid years of costly litigation should be applauded and rewarded. But bitter experience has trained many lawyers to believe that quick solutions don't impress their clients. They are used to being unknowingly encouraged by their clients to promote confrontation by being unnecessarily belligerent.

Who wins as a result of this behavior? Not the business owner, for the most part. The longer the legal proceedings, the more hours the lawyers rack up, and the higher the client's risk that something could go wrong.

3. "This is so simple, I could have written it myself."

Michael Jordan made scoring look so simple that it was easy to forget how skilled he was. He often looked like a man playing with boys. The same is true of the great athletes in any sport.

However, some business owners often look at simple, clearly written documents with disdain. They reason that because it says exactly what the business owner intended when making the deal, it could have been written by anyone. When people read this kind of document, it's easy for them to conclude that they could have saved the legal fees by writing their own simple agreement.

Many business owners try this. They put the contract into their computer and then start making changes, not knowing the importance of some key words and not realizing the fuzziness of the language they have chosen. The unfortunate part of the situation is that it may take years before they know the magnitude of the problems they have created (and then they can blame the litigation lawyer for charging too much to enforce in court the self-drafted provisions).

Anyone who thinks that writing simple documents is easy is wrong. Many documents that look simple are much harder to write than complex documents. The best thing about simple documents is that because they are so easy to understand, they are much more readily enforced by judges.

Think twice before you complain about a lawyer's bill for writing a "simple" document. Long, complex, unreadable, ambiguous, and self-contradictory contracts that are filled with far too many words like "wherefore," "heretofore," and "whereas" always look impressive because you cannot imagine ever being able to write them yourself. But before you complain about your lawyer's bill for writing a clear, readable, logical, and seemingly simple contract, think about what you are motivating your lawyer to deliver to you the next time you ask for help.

4. "I thought you were on my side."

People don't like to be told they are wrong—or that the law indicates that their prospects for success in a lawsuit are unpromising. This is especially true when strong emotions are involved. Sometimes you may suffer monetary loss, emotional pain, or betrayal and there may be nothing you can do about it. The best advice is to move on. As passionately as you might want revenge or vindication, and as convinced as you are from television or movies that a courtroom is where you will get it, there are times when it is highly unlikely or simply not possible.

An irate client once called me, demanding that I sue his accounting firm because they had ignored an IRS problem and, as a result, the IRS issued an otherwise uncalled-for levy that temporarily ruined his credit. Even though he owed the taxes and penalties that the IRS was claiming, he wanted the accounting firm to stall the date when payment would be required because he needed the cash for his business. The accountant's inattention destroyed his ability to persuade the IRS to give him a payment plan. All I had to do was tell him what he wanted to hear—that he should sue the accountants—and he would have hired me and I would have made a lot of money. Instead, I told him that suing would almost certainly be a futile waste of his money and that he should use his time, energy, and money on something more likely to be productive.

Fortunately, I had known this business owner for well over twenty years and he knew that I always tried to tell him what was best for him. However, I have had the experience of telling other clients that the revenge or vindication they wanted was not possible through the legal system, and then being told by those people that they felt I was not "on their side."

But when I think that filing a lawsuit is not my client's best option, or is not a realistic option at all, I remain quick to tell my clients, hopeful that they will appreciate both my candor and my willingness to pass up a chance to take their money.

Think of it this way. All lawyers, not just the "rainmakers" or managing partners, are salesmen. No one would doubt the advice of any other salesmen who tell you not to buy their products, even though you may want to. Ultimately, if you discourage your lawyer from giving honest advice and encourage him or her merely to be your cheerleader, don't expect to get honest advice in the future.

How to Spot Undesirable Legal Advice

"But," you might ask, "since some lawyers really are too timid, really do overcharge for writing simple documents, and really are not capable of writing documents that cover a complex transaction, how will I know that I am talking to a good business lawyer once I have found him or her?"

Unfortunately, there is no foolproof test. But if you try to recognize and avoid the people who *don't* qualify, you will almost certainly learn to identify the qualities of those who should qualify.

What are the signs you should look for to disqualify someone?

Beware of lawyers who make fighting seem like fun.

It's easy and, unfortunately, all too common for lawyers to play up the glamour of confrontation, pour salt on wounds, and stir up bruised emotions. They'll say things like, "We aren't going to let them push you around like this and play you for a fool," or, "We'll teach them a lesson!" Lawyers who glamorize the idea of being gunslingers or street-fighters either are used to pandering to your emotions in the hopes of fooling you into hiring them, or simply don't understand that the legal system is subtle and complex and rarely rewards bluster or intimidation.

Beware of lawyers who brag about their win-loss record.

Lawyers are not basketball coaches. Each situation is unique and the value of the lawyer's advice is most often not reflected by the number of cases they have won or lost or the size of the last deal they claim to have handled. A very skilled lawyer will often "win" most of his or her cases through settlement, an event that does not lend itself to a statistic.

Beware of lawyers who act like you are their employee.

When a lawyer tells you, "I never would let a client of mine do that," he or she is crossing an important line. After all, it's your problem, it's your business, it's your money, it's your future at stake. Who is the lawyer to "not allow" you to do something? The lawyer's job is to identify the potential risks and rewards of a course of action, and offer alternatives that have less risk or more potential reward.

Some lawyers, however, feel that their job is to simply protect you from risk, and some business owners actually tell the lawyer that this is what they want. Remember that your lawyers are your advisors. Presumably you can make the hard decisions about alternative courses of action better than your lawyer. Hiring a lawyer who thinks that it is his or her job to make these decisions for you is usually a bad idea.

Beware of lawyers who use complicated jargon.

Simple, straightforward English is always the best way to communicate. Is it really better to talk about your "internal ROI" than it is to discuss the "expected rate of return on your investment"? Is it better to say, "We'll sue in the Chancery court for an equitable writ of replevin," or simply, "We'll file a suit to get your property back"? Lawyers resort to legal or financial jargon for several reasons. Sometimes it's because they are smart and talented but simply are unable to communicate using simple English. Sometimes it's because they think that you will be impressed if they use esoteric phrases. Sometimes it's because they are so impressed by themselves that it makes them feel good to use the complicated language that impresses everyone at a dinner party. And sometimes it's simply a way to cover up for their own inability to understand the subject matter. But no matter what the reason, the result is poor communication, and that's never good.

Beware of lawyers who can't write clearly.

If you can't readily understand your lawyer's documents, it's reasonable to assume that no one else will either. Documents are not valuable if they do not communicate clearly. They should explain and clarify—never confuse. Yes, many transactions are very complicated and can only be described with many words. The documents used in bond financing transactions are good examples. They are complex transactions that are done best with complex documents. But, if there is a dispute, those thousands of words will have to be read and interpreted by a judge whose background before becoming a judge probably was not municipal finance, but rather criminal or matrimonial law. He or she may be very smart and hardworking, but, even so, the likelihood of documents being enforced by the judge as they were intended increases if they are written in the clearest and simplest possible way.

Beware of lawyers whose values don't reflect yours.

It's okay if you and your lawyer don't share political views, religious belief, or similar positions on gun control, welfare reform, or abortion. But it is important that the two of you share values such as honesty in negotiations and willingness to bluff.

Lawyers see all types of situations and deal with all types of people. Some lawyers think honesty is not only the best policy, but the only policy. Other lawyers avoid candor at all costs. Some lawyers feel that negotiations are best done using logic. Others believe in intimidation, obfuscation, and dissembling. Some lawyers assume that everyone is honest and forthright, while others assume that everyone is dishonest and overwhelmingly motivated by greed.

Various types of lawyers can find success using their principles, values, and assumptions. Although it is always a good idea to be suspicious, and it is sometimes helpful to get a second opinion from your lawyer on what people are *really* saying, make sure that you are getting a second opinion from someone you believe to be rational and perceptive, rather than merely being impressive because they are well educated and comfortably situated in a lavish office. In business, it is a bad idea both to trust no one and to trust everyone. There's no question it's naive to deny there are people who lie, cheat, and steal. However, being too suspicious can lead to your behaving in a way that makes you seem untrustworthy.

One of the skills of a good lawyer is to know when to trust and when to distrust. Ultimately, the lawyer does not own your business, and you, as the business owner, must be responsible for your own decisions. But a good lawyer should offer you advice that serves as a counterpoint to your judgment.

Beware the limitations of expertise

There is no question that when you have heart surgery, you do not want it done by someone who has never previously performed the procedure. On the other hand, as someone once said, "When a hammer is your only tool, every problem looks like a nail." Experts are often limited by their expertise such that they fail to see solutions that may appear to others.

For example: A lawyer who has gone to trial on many cases involving disputes with minority shareholders may get lost in the minutiae of dealing with valuation and not see opportunities to resolve the dispute with less legal expenses, less exposure to risk, and a better net result through compromise.

How to Deal with a Problem Lawyer

What should you do if you don't have a lawyer who adds value? When you have a lawyer whose honesty you trust, but who still can't communicate clearly?

Simple. You apply the same management techniques you would use in the other aspects of your business. When you have an employee or supplier who isn't performing satisfactorily, you have three choices. You either train them to perform to your expectations, find a new one who already has been trained that way, or live with mediocrity.

The easy (and most expensive) solution is, obviously, to live with mediocrity.

The solution that is both hardest yet best for you and your business is to train the lawyer to fit your need—or to find a new one who does.

The first step in training your lawyer is to make your expectations clear. If you had paper suppliers who were supplying you with the wrong type of paper, you would first explain what you needed and give them a chance to understand and fulfill your needs. If they didn't, you would know that you had to shop to find a new supplier.

Managing lawyers is no different. They are suppliers of a service. True, it's a very complicated service that is extremely difficult to produce. Yet it is, in fact, still a service. As with most services, in order to get what you want you need to spend time explaining your needs.

Don't be shy. If the problem is your lawyers' lack of clarity, tell them to start speaking in plainer English. Stop them each time they say something that you don't understand (and don't let them charge you extra for their struggle). Be explicit about whatever you see as the problem. Tell them to write clearer documents. Tell them to stop agreeing with you all the time and insist that they offer alternatives. Tell them to stop making the business decisions that should properly be yours to make.

If that doesn't work, you need to go shopping. If you do, you may be pleasantly surprised to find that the increasing competition among lawyers is starting to produce lawyers who truly understand the concept of value-added lawyering.

A Few Words on Paying Legal Fees

Once you view your lawyer as a supplier—as you should—you will begin to understand that, like any supplier, lawyers will be motivated both positively and negatively depending on the way you choose to pay their bills.

In fact, your fee-paying practices may actually dictate the kind of advice that you get from your lawyer.

An example: let's say you hire a lawyer to help you buy a factory building and decide to pay only if that transaction closes. That may seem like a good decision on your part because you expect it to motivate your lawyer to avoid raising "unnecessary" problems that just lengthen the negotiations, increase his time, and thus increase the bill. But in reality this fee structure rarely works to the advantage of the business owner. The idea of paying a fee only if the transaction closes not only announces to lawyers that you don't trust them, but it also gives them an incentive to do as little work as possible. As a result, they might ignore as much as is conscionable any problems that might make the transaction a bad deal for you. You have structured your lawyer's compensation so that it will be higher if he or she can close the deal with little or no work, even if that means that the lawyer needs to minimize or ignore environmental problems, defects in title, or the unwillingness of the seller to give important and typical warranties. Congratulations: You have motivated your lawyer to close the transaction without regard to your best interests and to do as little work as possible in the process.

Negotiating for a rate reduction if a transaction does not proceed has the same problems. It ignores the fact that quite often there are very good reasons why the transaction came to a halt. Punishing the lawyer for a job well done is neither fair nor good business.

With lawyers whose integrity you do not completely trust, you have two choices. You can either attempt to outsmart them through a compensation system, or you can run from them as quickly as possible and find someone you can trust. In the long run, a dishonest or untrustworthy lawyer will probably out-connive you the majority of the time. The real solution is to find honest people who understand that they must deliver value in exchange for being paid.

Like any supplier, lawyers will be motivated according to your practices with regard to how you pay their charges. Paying bills late probably will result in your telephone calls being returned late or your work being done only after the work of the prompt-paying clients has been completed and your lawyer has no other work waiting.

The Myth of Lower Hourly Fees

Imagine for a moment that you have chosen a doctor who will perform your open-heart surgery. Shortly before the operation the doctor announces to you that he is working with a resident who is four or five years out of medical school and, although the senior doctor is going to coach the resident very carefully, this resident will be doing all the work. "The advantage," says the senior doctor, "is that the bill will be cheaper because the resident charges a lower rate, and there's nothing to worry about since I will be looking over the resident's shoulder."

This situation is not dissimilar to your asking a senior lawyer, who charges $350 per hour, to have his associate, usually a young lawyer four or five years out of law school, do the work at a lower hourly rate, but with a great deal of supervision.

Although there are exceptions (most notably in litigation), this situation rarely works to the client's advantage. A senior lawyer often can do the job much more quickly and efficiently and, even though the hourly rate is higher, the total cost is ultimately less. Imagine that the project is to write a purchase contract for real estate. It is not unusual for senior lawyers, billing $350 per hour, to do this kind of project in two hours or less. After all, they have done many of these and they are very familiar with the form with which the drafting begins. On the other hand, if the work is assigned to junior lawyers, these younger, less experienced people may spend up to three hours on the same project, and the senior lawyers will then have to spend at least a half hour reviewing the work. And it's all too common for the senior lawyer to make compromises in quality so as not to diminish the junior lawyer's enthusiasm. The math is simple: two hours at $350 per hour is far less than three hours at $250 per hour plus a half hour at $350.

How Much Should You Pay Your Lawyer?

Yes, lawyers charge a lot of money. Attorney fees can be $200, $300, $400 per hour, or more—anywhere from about $3 a minute to over $10 a minute. And that may not even include expenses.

Those minutes or hours add up quickly. So, how can you control your legal fees? It's a good question. Here's a way to formulate an answer.

The real issue should never be about what you're paying. It should be about what you're getting. You're being charged for a lawyer's time, and for that you should receive substantial results.

Several years ago, I tried to negotiate the hourly fees of an expert who my client was about to hire. The expert, an older man, told me a story about a man who owned a company whose business depended on highly complex computers. One day, in the middle of a job, the company's computers would not operate and the company had to shut down. The owner called in the outside computer experts he had dealt with and, although they immediately came out to his plant, after twenty-four hours of tinkering they couldn't get the machinery operating again. He then tried another set of experts who were equally unsuccessful.

He was understandably frantic. He then tried a man whose name he had been given by another business owner. This man came to his factory, walked around for a few minutes, then took out a small screwdriver and turned a small screw. Then he said, "Try the machines, they should work now."

The owner tried the machines and, as predicted, they were all working. The computers were humming away like new. He asked for the bill, which came out to $10,000. Shocked, the owner said, "$10,000! You were only here fifteen minutes, how did you compute that bill?"

The man smiled and said, "For turning the screw, I charged $200 dollars an hour. That's $50. I charged $9,950 for knowing which screw to turn."

For lots of reasons, lawyers overcharge for the screw-turning and undercharge for knowing which screw to turn. To manage your lawyers most effectively, you need to be able to distinguish between paying for labor and paying for creative solutions.

Before you feel cheated by overcharging, make sure you have not had the advantage of having been undercharged for knowing which screw to turn. A lawyer may not really be worth $400 per hour just for dictating a letter, but if that letter contains an artfully drafted phrase that gets a $100,000 deadbeat account to pay in full, a business owner who felt he was overcharged is ignoring the incredible value that the lawyer brings by knowing which screw to turn.

If you want to save the cash going toward a lawyer's hourly rate, don't hire one. It's as simple as that. But, is it worth the risk? You—and only you—need to make that decision. It's *your* responsibility to manage your legal fees.

Most people think that the best way to save money with lawyers is to negotiate hourly fees. They assume that if they can get a $350 per hour attorney to work for "only" $300 an hour, they'll save more. To them, it's a simple matter of math. Every hour that a lawyer works on their behalf, they "save" $50.

But law isn't mathematics. Not by a long shot.

Look at it this way. You can negotiate price with any of your vendors. But even if they agree to cut costs, they often make up for those cuts in other ways. Sometimes it may be speed of delivery, sometimes it may be the quality of the product, and sometimes it may be the way they treat their business relationship with you.

In business, you never want to be a patsy. You never want to overpay—especially if you're buying a commodity. But when you're seeking a unique non-commodity service, the correlation between the cost and value is more obscure.

Put another way, how much would you want to save on your heart surgeon?

Money doesn't necessarily buy quality. Then again, the best quality and sometimes even the best value are rarely available at discount prices. What's more, if you're really concerned about money, negotiating hourly fees with an attorney is probably the worst way to accomplish your goal.

Why? Well, there are lots of reasons. Here's one: Let's say you hire a highly respected lawyer who charges $500 per hour. She spends a few hours with you, hears your concerns and frustrations, makes a few suggestions, and together you agree on a goal. Then she makes one phone call to another equally powerful attorney and they reach an agreement. It's done quickly, efficiently, and at a far lower cost to you than hiring a $200/hour attorney who might spend weeks and weeks earnestly working in your best interests, but never getting helpful results.

Here are some others: You feel proud of yourself for having negotiated that $50 hourly savings with your lawyer. Now, ask yourself one question: who's keeping track of the hours? Or, to put it another way, what is that lawyer's motivation to work quickly and efficiently in your behalf? Whose work will your lawyer do first—yours or that of the clients paying full price? Do you really want someone negotiating *for* you who is not smart enough to negotiate successfully *with* you?

Frankly, a lawyer's hourly charges are a relatively minor issue. Out of the total budget for your business, legal fees represent only a tiny portion. No matter how well you negotiate the fees, you really aren't likely to reduce that percentage by much.

This is not to say that you should pay anything a lawyer asks. And no one should ever suggest that the lawyers who bill at the highest rates are the best lawyers. There is a market for legal services, and there is no reason to pay more than that market requires. There may be no need to pay a large retainer simply because a lawyer requests one. Most business lawyers in large cities will give their clients credit. As with any service, the goal when paying lawyers is not to squeeze out the lowest possible price, but to get the best combination of price and valuable service.

Four

Litigation and Compromise— It's Not About Justice, It's About Dollars

Few situations faced by business owners evoke more emotional turmoil and result in more needlessly wasted money, time, and energy than litigation. This is especially true when the litigation combines business disagreements with family dynamics. As is the case in almost all situations involving disappointment, anger, the risk of losing large amounts of money, or complicated emotions, litigation almost always leads to large and unnecessary expenditures; inordinate amounts of time directed away from the business; and the inevitable exposure of the business to additional risk.

Fortunately, this does not have to be the case. But avoiding the traps created by uncontrolled emotions or frustrated expectations requires that you do the following:

- understand the nature of the litigation process;
- set achievable goals;
- don't overestimate your lawyer's power or wisdom;
- don't underestimate the time you'll need to spend away from your buisness; and
- don't overestimate the magnitude of the problems you hope the litigation will address.

Readjust Your Concept

Many people naively think of litigation as a process that determines who is "right" and who is "wrong," who is "guilty" and who is "innocent," who is lying and who is telling the truth.

Or, to put it more simply, many people think that the litigation process dispenses "justice."

Unfortunately, the legal system is designed to do something slightly less ambitious and grandiose: to resolve disputes based on the application of rules—rules that are uniform and as consistently applied as humans are capable of doing. However, any person who has been wrongfully accused to their mother by their brother or sister quickly learns that no dispute resolution system is perfect.

Imagine for a minute the characteristics of the perfect dispute resolution system. Each party would have the money to employ a team of the best possible lawyers. These lawyers would then spend whatever time was necessary to uncover all of the available evidence, conduct extensive interviews of all of the available witnesses, uncover all the applicable laws and thoroughly research all of the past legal precedents. Before the trial, the lawyers would conduct a mock trial in front of a mock jury to determine how witnesses could best phrase their testimony and how lawyers could best phrase their arguments to be as clear and persuasive as possible. The case would then be presented to the smartest judge, who would then write a lengthy report of his or her logic and conclusions. The losing side could then appeal the case to the brightest and most sensitive panel of appellate court judges and, if necessary, to the Supreme Court.

The advantage of this perfect system is that it would deliver the highest quality of justice. The disadvantage is that it would be absurdly time-consuming and expensive for the participants.

In the United States, our government provides many different dispute resolution systems. All fifty states and the federal government have courts with their own unique rules. But as different as they all are, they abound with similarities. The greatest similarity is also the one most often overlooked—despite how often people may talk about how "the system" is broken, every one of these systems resolves every dispute. They may do it more slowly or at a higher expense than most people like, and they may encourage compromise more aggressively than most people like, but in 100 percent of the cases the dispute is resolved. The system works, even though in almost all of the cases that go to trial, the losers—50 percent of the participants—are disappointed.

The reality, which almost everyone who deals with our legal system eventually understands, is that anyone who does not like the system always has the alternative of resolving the dispute by reaching a voluntary compromise, or settlement, with the opposing party. When business owners think of a dispute only in terms of right or wrong or being just or unjust, or as a test of their character or values, they are adopting a paradigm that is completely incongruous with the real-life system in which they are operating. To make a dispute into a test of character, a validation of one's principles, or an opportunity to affirm one's righteousness is to destroy the opportunity for reaching a compromise that saves money, saves time, and avoids the risk of losing more of both if the decision is not in your favor. In other words, an approach that prevents a business owner from seeing the dispute as one about money is an approach that often leads to disappointment and unnecessary monetary risk.

For example, if someone acknowledges that a particular dispute involves only $5,000, he will form a mental budget of how much money can be spent to resolve the dispute favorably. No one involved in a dispute over $5,000 would rationally spend $15,000 on legal fees in order to win the case.

On the other hand, if the same dispute is not about $5,000, but rather about "integrity," "courage," or worse, some adolescent view of "manhood," then an investment of $15,000 in legal fees, or even $150,000 in legal fees, begins to make sense. After all, the value of the victory or the consequence of a loss is priceless. The lawyer is effectively given a blank check to spend as much money as necessary to accomplish the affirmation of these larger principles that override money.

There is nothing wrong in a moral or ethical sense about viewing disputes as moral or ethical battles. But be warned: it is almost always economically unwise.

Virtually all business owners realize that in many situations, doing good business does not require being right. Many believe that in business the issue of right or wrong is predetermined—*the customer* is always right. Years ago, I was waiting for a clerk in a large department store. The woman in front of me was returning a set of glass salt and pepper shakers. She innocently explained to the clerk that this was a wedding present she had received that arrived broken in the mail. The saleswoman cheerfully did what the store was famous for—she took back the items and gave the customer a full credit with a smile and without a question. After the woman in front of me had walked out of earshot, the saleswoman mumbled to me that the items could not have been broken in shipment—after all, there was still salt and pepper in the shakers.

This department store did not resolve this dispute based on the moral principle of being right, or of not rewarding liars. Rather, the issue was resolved by applying the principle that had made the store successful: happy customers are loyal customers who will come back and spend more money. Rather than rigidly clinging to particular principles, the store's managers set a policy that would preserve both customers' happiness and employees' time.

Yes, of course the people on the other side are not customers and making them happy is of no value. But that is not the point! The point is that disputes, whether with customers, shareholders, vendors, or employees, are often best resolved by determining what is best for the business, and not by the rigid application of moral principles.

Don't Let a Lawsuit Turn Your World Upside Down

Business owners all too often turn litigation into an emotional issue rather than one of business. Litigation then becomes a confrontation between good (you) and evil (others), as opposed to merely a process for defining and resolving business disputes. Getting overwhelmed by the emotions that are stirred up by a conflict is generally worse for the business than losing the dispute.

Business owners should never let disputes blind them to the fact that they are running businesses. Objectivity is required; without it a business owner can't make informed decisions about any issue, especially litigation. The cost of losing objectivity will (unless dumb luck intervenes) invariably end up being measured in large sums of money.

People do bad things to each other, in business as in other endeavors: they lie, they cheat, they go back on their word.

But is the business best served by pursuing the goal of revenge? Shouldn't business owners think twice before investing their valuable time, and their companies' money, on legal fees that serve no purpose other than satisfying their need for vengeance? Shouldn't the real issue be the success of the business?

Risk—The Ever-Changing Calculation

In the context of a lawsuit, there are two particularly important aspects of risk that need to be understood.

- Every lawsuit involves risk.
- A lawsuit only occurs once.

Why are these so important?

Imagine that you meet a man who makes the following proposal: "I will put $250 on the table, and you put $50 on the table. I flip a coin and the winner takes all the money." Anyone faced with this opportunity will do it as often as possible. You have a 50/50 chance of winning 500 percent of your potential losses. If you can do it a few hundred thousand times, you are sure to become rich. Not even monumental bad luck will defeat the reality that if you flip this coin enough times, you will win enough money so that you will probably never have to work again. Yes, there is a slight theoretical risk that you will end up losing, but almost no one would refuse to take this bet.

Now imagine that you meet the same man, who makes the same proposal, but with just two significant changes. First, instead of your putting $50 on the table, you need to put on the table every single asset that you have to your name—your house, your cars, your children's trust funds, your savings account, your retirement accounts, and your business. So, instead of betting $50, you are now betting *everything that you have*.

Yes, the man will match it by 500 percent, no matter how much money that is.

But, instead of being able to do this as many times as you want, this opportunity will only happen *once*. If you correctly guess the coin flip, your wealth will increase fivefold. But if you guess wrong, you and your family will be penniless and homeless, you will have no job, and you will have no chance to ever take the bet again.

Same odds, same payoff. Yet, the *risk* of the second proposition is infinitely higher than that of the first.

Lawsuits are similar: they all involve risk and they all only occur once. They may or may not require that you put all your wealth at risk, but many lawsuits require that you risk what an accountant might call a "material" amount.

To make wise decisions, you must understand the situation you are facing. That means you must fully understand the magnitude of the risk of losing—no matter how "right" you might be, there is *always* a risk of losing—and come to grips with the fact that this bet will never occur again.

Don't Create Meaningless Metaphors

Many business owners persist in thinking that a lawsuit is a test of their values, culture, or principles. And the lawyers for these business owners invariably make huge amounts of money when their clients think, "If I pay even 30 percent of this crummy piece-of-garbage claim to this incompetent supplier, every one of my vendors who ever messes up is going to sue me for money they are not entitled to. I need to use this case to teach 'the marketplace' and my children that I have principles, that I will not give in to this kind of legal blackmail."

It is not a lawyer's role to decide for clients how to deal with these emotional issues. But a good lawyer should point out the two fallacies of making business decisions from this emotional, and not a business, point of view.

First, there are no guarantees about the outcome of a lawsuit. The side that is "right" does not always win. Sometimes the participants in the system, the judge or the jury, make mistakes. And second, a company's suppliers, vendors, and customers are generally too preoccupied with their own problems to worry about how you resolved a dispute or to take the high-stakes gamble of using that resolution as a way to take advantage of you. The truth is that "the marketplace" rarely learns about the terms on which a lawsuit was settled.

Of course, every once in a while, a business owner is faced with a situation that really does have metaphorical import, and defending that lawsuit is important for deterring future lawsuits. Typically, how a business deals with discrimination claims from employees who are fired (especially from those against whom it did *not* discriminate) may, in fact, have repercussions in terms of how some subsequently fired employees will react. But that does not mean that how a business owner deals with a dispute with a vendor or shareholder will affect how other vendors or shareholders deal with that business owner.

Nor should a business owner always view compromises with family members as showing a weakness that others will exploit. Having a cousin/shareholder leave to go into competition is, in reality, probably a once-in-a-lifetime experience and will seem far less attractive to other shareholders if that cousin's business fails, as most startups do. Risking a huge amount of money to establish a "principle" has little justification if the situation has little likelihood of recurring.

Don't Kill the Messenger

Have you ever been lucky enough to have a saleswoman who told you the suit you liked didn't make you look good? If you have, you didn't accuse her of "being afraid to sell you that suit." You didn't accuse her of "not being on your side." Chances are you thanked her for her courage and honesty. But almost all lawyers have had the experience of being scorned, yelled at, or fired by a client to whom they made recommendations like "don't sue," or "just pay off the claim and go on to other issues," or "compromise."

Lawyers should be thought of as service providers who supply litigation. They rarely "sell" litigation like someone sells a highly polished used car. But, nevertheless, like any salesman, if you purchase their services in conducting litigation, they will make money.

And, like any other salesperson, if they are advising a prospective customer (you) not to buy the product or service they are paid to sell (litigation), it is almost invariably well-intentioned advice. It may not always be good advice, but it is almost never given out of cowardice or weakness. Even if the advice is disappointing, a business owner should take time to consider it and calmly decide if it is rational.

Of course, filing or fighting a lawsuit is often the best way to resolve a dispute. And sometimes it may be inappropriate for lawyers to tell their clients to avoid a lawsuit. Sometimes the more cautious lawyer really is wrong and the more aggressive lawyer is giving the better advice. But even in those instances when cautious lawyers may not possess the best judgment, they should be respected for giving courageous and honest advice.

Trials—Hardly an Exact Science

Why is it that business owners should be so aware of the risk of losing at a trial when they *know* the truth? After all, they were there! They saw what happened! They have witnesses! And their very well-educated and successful lawyer has done research and found that there are cases exactly on point. How can they *possibly* lose if there is a fair trial?

Unfortunately, just as there are no sure investments in the stock market, so, too, are there no sure things in lawsuits. Why?

- "The Law" is not a simple set of clear rules. If the law were simple, hundreds of thousands of lawyers wouldn't be able to charge so much money to argue about it. For each of your on-point cases, the other side will produce a case suggesting that you are wrong and will, with a straight face, explain to the judge why the cases your lawyer uses are not on point.

- Like all other people, judges and juries make mistakes.
- Key witnesses may be unavailable. They may die, move away, forget, or even lie.
- In real life, it is almost never easy to prove that something is a lie. A trial is not a scripted drama where the lawyer traps the witness who then breaks down and tearfully admits to lying. Some people are very skillful at lying. They could sell ice to Icelanders. Even if you tell the truth and your opponent lies, the judge might not believe you.
- You may be right, but have no evidence other than your own testimony.
- Your "witnesses" may have lied to you to cover up their mistakes.
- Even written documents may prove to be ambiguous.
- The "truth" is usually very, very hard to determine in absolute terms. Two people may genuinely and honestly have differing understandings of the same conversation or event.

Everyone who has been involved in litigation eventually comes to see it as a good news, bad news situation. The bad news is that if any dispute is to be resolved by someone else (a judge or jury, or even a caring mother), it is not possible to guarantee the outcome.

But the good news is that, as uncertain as you may be about the eventual outcome, it is equally certain that the other party is just as uncertain.

Under these circumstances, a compromise that reflects the risk to *both* sides is a rational and ultimately the most likely outcome. The results of almost every study done of business disputes show that more than 95 percent of the lawsuits are voluntarily settled without a trial. This means that over 95 percent of the participants realize that a trial is just not a good idea—it's too risky, too expensive, and too time-consuming.

Settlements Are *Not* Losses

In order to make wise decisions about when to settle or what to settle for, a business owner must avoid believing in some very expensive myths about settlements. Settlements are not failures. Settlements are not signs of weakness. Settlements are not evidence of poor leadership. Settlements are not defeats. Settlements, if done at the right time and for the right amount, are victories.

Unfortunately, some lawyers don't understand the wisdom of settlements. It is all too common for lawyers to ask their client in litigation, "Do you want to settle?" Predictably, most business owners respond honestly, "No!" and the discussion, unfortunately, ends.

This lawyer's poorly phrased question led to an honest but ill-advised answer. Desire is never the issue! No one wants to settle, because no one likes to compromise. But almost every case should be settled! Every rational business owner should devise a strategy to settle, even though most don't like the idea.

And, by devising a settlement strategy, you can take control and help your lawyer add value. If your lawyer asks you if you want to settle, your reply should *always* be, "What do you think is a good strategy to reach a settlement that is good for me in terms of my risks, my potential expenses, and my potential benefits?" By asking the question, "Do you want to settle?" the lawyer is avoiding the more difficult question that results in the more valuable answer: "At what price should a rational settlement occur?"

Business owners sometimes forget to ask that question because of the negative connotations of the word *settlement*. Wise business leaders should deal with litigation by addressing the same question they would ask before making any major business decision: "In view of the risks involved, is my projected investment of time and money wise in terms of the likely gain [if you are trying to get someone else to pay you money] or reduction of loss [if you are trying to avoid paying someone else money] and the risks involved?"

Once the issue is framed as a business decision, the business owner can begin to develop an intellectual framework to confront the real business questions presented by litigation. Questions like, is it better to accept $200,000 as a compromise for a $400,000 claim, or to invest a nonrefundable $75,000 in legal fees (and a great deal of company staff time) to have a trial where there is a 50/50 chance of winning? Or, should I pay $70,000 to a vendor who delivered goods that didn't meet my specifications, or $55,000 to a lawyer (and several days of your time) to have a trial where I have a 20 percent chance of losing $200,000?

Trials are certainly more thrilling than settlements and, if you win, always give you interesting stories to tell at dinner parties or to the person sitting next to you on a long airplane flight. But that does not make them good business decisions.

Settlements are not defeats, even though they might feel that way. Part of the problem is that many business owners and certainly most entrepreneurs are intensely competitive. Their egos and emotions ride on results. To them, a settlement is the emotional equivalent of going for a tie instead of a win. But, overcoming this thought pattern is, in the long run, good for their business.

A Simple Guide to Successful Settlements

It was von Clausewitz, the great German military theorist, who observed that "War is a continuation of diplomacy by other means." The same idea was expressed more colorfully by a Chicago police officer I once heard quoted as saying, "It's much easier to get things done with a smile and a gun, than with just a smile."

It should only take a moment's thought to appreciate the wisdom of these statements. A diplomat cannot negotiate a successful resolution of an international dispute without the ability to wage war or to repel an invader. And the threat of war is an essential tool for diplomats to use in reaching a "diplomatic" resolution. Since

World War II, almost all of the wars have ended with a diplomatic resolution rather than surrenders and victory marches through the capitals of vanquished enemies. A diplomatic solution—a ceasefire or truce—is based on the mutually perceived benefit to each side of avoiding the mutual destruction that will occur if war is pursued. Few would say that the United States' effort to liberate Kuwait from Iraq was a defeat merely because it ended in a diplomatic settlement. One can argue that the diplomatic solution was reached too early or too late, but almost no one would perceive the ending of this dispute as a defeat.

Similarly, business owners make the most rational and efficient decisions by understanding litigation as a continuation of a negotiation and not the end of a negotiation. There is no reason to think of litigating and negotiating as mutually exclusive.

Most people (lawyers included) view litigation as a process of preparing for and then pursuing a trial. But the data shows that in all but a few rare instances, *litigation is a process of preparing for and pursuing a settlement.* More than 95 percent of business lawsuits are resolved by compromise.

What does this mean? In most cases, you should look at litigation as a means of preparing for a settlement. Not only is this view much more realistic, but it also allows business owners to see the process in a way that will help them get better results, i.e. a process of persuading the other side to reach a compromise to your advantage.

This requires you to redefine what it means to "win." Watch a business trial and you will see that they are often mundane and boring. They usually have to do with matters like who promised what to whom, what a poorly written contract was intended to mean when it was signed four years earlier, or what a particular industry's custom is regarding how many units belong in a box.

The smart business approach to litigation means, first and foremost, planning what happens during pretrial activities in order to enhance settlement negotiations. Getting 70 percent of a claim that you only had a 50/50 chance of winning is a real victory. Going to trial on a claim that you have a 50/50 chance of winning after you were offered a settlement of 70 percent may not be losing, but since it requires taking on more risk, it probably is not smart.

Never lose sight of a basic principle: it's not about justice, it's about getting the best net results. These are often measurable in dollars.

"Well," you might say, "all that is good, but how do I get *them* to compromise when their lawyer says they want a trial?"

First, avoid the common traps that impede compromise and send your legal costs skyrocketing:

1. *Don't get mad, except on purpose.* Anger will almost always overwhelm good judgment. Not only that, it can also overwhelm the other party's good judgment, too. You and your lawyers can very easily make your opponents so angry that they decide they want to fight to the death. In those instances, the war continues and the legal costs escalate. You may have enjoyed the drama of making them angry, but it is almost always expensive theater. A show of anger may have strategic value in a negotiation. But giving full rein to your anger may escalate feelings on both sides beyond the point at which you can hope to strike a compromise before trial.

2. *Don't negotiate against yourself.* If you make an offer, don't sweeten it until your opponent has made a counteroffer. If you increase the amount of your offer (or decrease the amount of your demand) without any movement from the other side, your action will—and should—be viewed as a sign that you have lost either your confidence or your patience. Once the other side realizes this, they will try to see just how desperate or impatient you really are.

3. *Don't make an absurdly low offer.* In order to avoid having to negotiate against yourself, don't be so greedy that you make an offer to which the other side has no incentive to respond. Say, for example, that you offer 20 percent of what your opponents are asking, even

though you (and your opponents) know that you have a 60 percent chance of losing your case if it goes to trial. When your opponents don't respond, as they probably will not, you will then have no alternative but to sweeten your offer or else go to trial and spend more on legal fees. In effect, your strategy trapped you into negotiating against yourself.

4. *Don't be inflexible.* Don't make a "best-and-only" offer, thinking that it will somehow quickly resolve the dispute. If the other side has patience, they will not act quickly—certainly they will not act quickly just because you want them to. It may feel good to come off as "tough," but it usually prolongs lengthy back-and-forth negotiations. In reality, it puts you at a disadvantage, because your opponents can, by delaying, test whether they can get you to move from your "unmovable" position (and they probably will). This strategy locks you into a position that takes away your opportunity to hear your opponents' offer and try to get them to change it.

5. *Don't be insulted by the act of negotiating.* A very common mistake is to feel insulted if the other party disagrees with you. And, when that other side is made up of your family members, it is tempting to feel that they do not love, appreciate, or respect you. Negotiations among brothers, sisters, cousins, sons, or daughters often fail to reach agreement because the participants cannot overcome the feeling that their siblings or children are not sufficiently appreciative. A classic example often occurs in negotiating a buyout of a father's interest in a business. The father feels the business is worth $20 million. The child who is the designated successor feels the business is worth $10 million. The father becomes enraged and causes the negotiation to revolve around the value of "everything I've done for you," as opposed to the real issue, the current fair value of the business if

it were to be sold to a stranger. When you try to measure love, respect, or appreciation using money (always a bad idea), it's hard to negotiate a good resolution.

Of course, merely avoiding these common mistakes will not resolve a dispute. The best way to do that is by using a strategy.

Often, lawyers develop a strategy for a trial, but won't come up with a strategy for a settlement. This is, of course, shortsighted, since there is a 95 percent chance that most disputes will be settled before a trial. The sensible and practical approach is to develop a strategy that answers this question: "What can my lawyer and I do to persuade them to change their position?"

No simple answer to this question will apply to every case. Your job is to figure out what you and your lawyer can do in your particular case that will make the other side more willing to compromise. Consider: What are they thinking? What are they feeling? What are they spending?

You may not realize it—and your lawyer may not necessarily think in these terms—but the litigation process provides many tools and tactics you can use to persuade the other side to compromise. Not all can be used effectively in any one case. Not all can be used effectively at the same time. But your lawyer should know what these eleven tools and tactics can do, and how and when to use them.

1. *Let your actions speak louder than your words.* This is a fundamental rule of human behavior: what you do has more of an impact than what you say. For example, if you make a big concession early on, you cannot expect that the other side will believe you if you say that you are prepared to go to trial. But if your actions are consistent with your words—you say you're confident of winning and make only a modest settlement offer, or you say something is non-negotiable and you refuse to discuss it—you are more likely to convince your opponents.

2. *Get real.* Don't be afraid to admit to the other side that you are realistic. Your candor can lead to their being realistic, too. Admitting the obvious—that you realize that it's possible you might lose

a trial—often leads them to make the same admission, at which point everyone can discuss a resolution more realistically.

3. *Make them ask their lawyer for a prediction.* Often, people go to their lawyers wanting to sue someone who they feel has taken advantage of them, or because they are being sued by someone for a similar reason. In either case, they are probably both very upset and very afraid of losing. Normally, the clients tell their lawyers their stories and ask, "Do I have a case?" The answer is almost always, "Yes, if we can prove what you say, you will probably win." Many clients simply don't hear or understand this huge "if"; it's as though they only hear, "Yes...you will win!"

Of course, this common conversation totally avoids the more relevant question: "What are the *chances* of proving my case?" This is the question clients most often do not think to ask, and also the question that is most difficult for lawyers to answer. Many lawyers will only answer this question if they have to—if it is asked very clearly, very persistently, and very directly.

As a result, one very effective way to bring about a settlement is to get the decision-makers on the other side to ask that question of their lawyers. The answer is usually quite sobering to the client and can often lead to a settlement within a few weeks.

4. *Keep them guessing.* Many people talk or think about lawsuits as if they were games. This is understandable, because there are many aspects of the process that are similar to games like chess or poker. Some business owners want their lawyers to simply tell the lawyers on the other side why they will lose, and naively think that this will result in a quick and favorable settlement. This is often a mistake. In litigation, as in poker, your opponents will often not fold simply because you have shown them the good cards in your hand. Once your opponents know your strengths (few people want to tell the other side about their weaknesses), they may simply respond by changing their arguments, strategies, briefs, and even their witnesses' testimony. In other words, knowledge is power, and by giving them more knowledge of your case you are giving them more power. Their lack of knowledge increases their risk of proceeding. Remember, two factors that

motivate compromise are expense and uncertainty. Keep them uncertain about your position.

5. *Change their risk/reward analysis—force them to invest more money.* Rational people involved in a dispute are constantly reevaluating the risk/reward analysis of their investment in attorneys' fees. After all, the ultimate goal is the best *net* result, and the lawyer's fees almost always reduce the net. In other words, if you are involved in a dispute with an unhappy customer who you feel owes you $50,000 and has offered you nothing, you should first ask your lawyer to assess the likelihood of your winning this dispute. Assume that your lawyer says you have a 60/40 chance. Under those circumstances, it is certainly rational to invest, say, $1,500 in attorney's fees to file the complaint. If you were in Las Vegas and were told that you had a 60/40 chance of winning $50,000 by betting $1,500, you would take the bet.

From your customer's point of view, once you have filed suit, offering you nothing becomes irrational. The customer might not cave in immediately, but they will probably offer something close to one-quarter or one-third of your demand before spending, say, the $2,000 of attorneys' fees necessary to prepare the response to a lawsuit in which they have a 40/60 bet. Even if they offer only $12,500 (one-quarter), you have just gotten a better than 800 percent return on your investment of $1,500 to file the complaint. Your decision to invest money required them to invest money. The reality of their having to make this investment led to their offering a settlement. Your investment changed the risk/reward analysis for them, a move that, in many cases, often leads to this kind of compromise offer.

6. *Disrupt their business.* When you formulate a settlement strategy, consider whether such things as depositions or the timing of a trial might interfere with your opponent's business. For instance, some industries involve critical trade shows. One case I handled was settled simply because the judge would not reschedule the trial to accommodate one party's need to attend their industry's annual trade show. Consider whether you can make their job of providing the discovery information you've requested so inconvenient that

they will agree to a more attractive settlement just to avoid the trouble.

7. *Be selectively silent.* As noted earlier, doing nothing *is* doing something. Silence disturbs many entrepreneurs. They feel compelled to respond immediately to all requests or settlement proposals. However, to not respond is to send a message. Always consider doing nothing after they make a move. It is often a very effective way to indicate that you are not interested in the steps they're taking to end the dispute. Not getting a response to a settlement proposal may, at first, disappoint or anger them. But, over time, their anger or disappointment may turn to insecurity caused by your being self-confident enough to remain silent. Impatience can cost you dearly.

8. *Know when time is on your side.* Time is almost always a factor in a lawsuit. In the simplest cases, the plaintiffs want money. Even though the defendants may have to pay something eventually, they would like to pay it as late as possible so that they can use it as working capital for as long as possible. Always be aware of whose side time is on. When time is on your side, allowing the litigation to drag on can convince your opponents that their strategy isn't working and may lead them to drop their expectations. Your delay can lead to their making an offer that is better for you.

9. *Make the dispute smaller, not larger.* This is one of the harder things to do. After all, who hasn't heard that the best defense is a good offense? Unfortunately, although that phrase is common wisdom to every American who loves sports, it is not wise in every situation. Thinking that the best defense is to attack, many people insist that their lawyers make disputes bigger. This is commonly done in three ways.

First, they ask for much more money than they could ever rationally expect to win at trial.

Second, they treat the other side in an insulting or demeaning manner. For some reason, they forget, or never believed in the first place, that the goal is to persuade the other side to compromise, and no one likes to compromise with people who have insulted them. Years ago, I worked for a lawyer who could be staggeringly impolite and demeaning. In the course of a lawsuit against a large, publicly held automobile company, he treated the company's president as if he were an idiot and a liar. Years later, I found out that the president of the company refused to settle for over a year and caused my boss's client to spend well over $100,000 of otherwise unnecessary legal fees—just because of my boss having insulted him.

Third, when a suit is filed, most business owners wish to file a countersuit even if it is virtually frivolous. Often, this kind of behavior results in a perverse win-win situation. The clients win because they are happier at being able to vent their anger, and the lawyers win because they become richer. What many people fail to realize is that this behavior does nothing more than create drama while making it harder to reach a rational resolution. Both insults and countersuits can certainly have their place. But like every strategy, they are not *always* the smart thing to do. Countersuits often make business owners feel good because they feel they are doing something positive and not merely defending themselves. Yes, they may sometimes bring about better settlements, but they almost never bring about better net results—they are often expensive, they can cause lengthy delays, and they sometimes (if too far-fetched) even result in court-ordered sanctions.

10. *Think of legal fees as an investment.* There is one sure rule of litigation: *all lawsuits can be settled in a heartbeat.* Give the other side what they want and they will *always* settle. But what they want may change from day to day, or week to week. Always be aware of the price (at that moment) that your opponents have put on a settlement. Once you know this, you should think of legal fees as an investment into changing that figure. Set investment goals. Assess the risks. Determine the other potential uses for that money. Do you want a 10-1 return, a 5-1 return, or a 1-1 return on the money you invest in your lawyer to change the other side's position? Can you get a better return for less risk by investing the money elsewhere in your business? Think of the process as one of making incremental investments based on the likelihood of achieving a goal. Think of legal fees as an investment into changing the status quo.

11. *Don't forget that your own time is money.* Lawsuits almost al-

ways take up a surprisingly large amount of a business owner's time and energy. Preparation for a three-hour deposition can take a full day. In some situations, producing documents can take several days. If you run a profitable business, this time can be used more productively. There are some situations where it is simply good business to pay more than what you think someone's claim is worth simply to be done with the time requirements of a lawsuit.

A good example of this happened to me a few years ago. My client, a toy company, had brought a suit for copyright infringement. The case raised a complicated question of law and we were not at all confident of winning. While the suit progressed, the alleged infringer had a new, unrelated product that began selling very well. After about a year, the alleged infringer's lawyer called and asked how much money we wanted to drop the lawsuit. My client named a price that was about 125 percent of the most I thought we could get at a trial. It was about twice what I knew we would have accepted. My client thought that this was a good place to start: a number that was not unreasonably high but still allowed plenty of space for negotiation. To my amazement, the defendant agreed to pay the full amount. Years later, the opposing lawyer from this case and I were invited to the same dinner party and we reminisced about some of the more interesting intellectual issues our case had presented. In the course of that discussion, this lawyer confirmed my suspicion: his client had knowingly overpaid my client, not because he was afraid of losing but because he needed to free up his time to devote himself to his hot-selling new product, which ended up making him one of the wealthiest men in America. His payment was a victory for us, but, more importantly, it was a bigger victory for him. He knew his time was worth more than the money he willingly overpaid us.

When to Settle?

If you find yourself embroiled in a lawsuit, the first step in deciding when and at what price to settle is to evaluate the costs, risks, and rewards, all while trying to predict what the other side might do. This is not easy.

Who should you go to for this information? Your lawyer. Will you get straight, clear answers? Maybe, maybe not. But this *should* be within your lawyer's expertise. After all, what should lawyers be good at, if not answering the hard questions? Why else are they getting those big bucks?

Some lawyers will be reluctant to try to answer these questions for two reasons. First, they may not have been trained to evaluate litigation in these terms, and therefore may be uncomfortable with them. If this is the case, insist that you get this service, and if you have a lawyer that won't give it, find a new lawyer who will.

Second, your lawyer may fear (probably based on experience with other, less-rational business owners) that you will hear these assessments as guarantees. This is understandable. It is your job to make sure your lawyer understands that you know you are not getting a guarantee and that you will not try to blame the lawyer if those assessments end up wrong. In other words, if you were to go to trial 10 times in a case where you have a 90 percent chance of winning, you *will* still lose once. And, when you do lose that one time, it is not your lawyer's fault!

You may need to persist in order to pin down your lawyer's honest and candid predictions. And don't blame your lawyer if those predictions change. People *should* learn more as time goes on. Additional knowledge and information about a situation *should* change how that situation is evaluated. Good investment advisors might recommend that you buy a stock during one month and then suggest you sell it a few months later. Similarly, you want lawyers who feel free to change their recommendations to fit changes in the known facts. Certainly, no one benefits if you unwittingly coerce your lawyers into changing the facts so that they fit their original recommendations.

Keep asking the following questions of your lawyer (and yourself), and make sure you have clear answers:

- "If I proceed with the case, what do you estimate will be the additional required investment in legal fees?"

Remember, what you've already spent is gone. The price at which you bought a stock is irrelevant to its current value. Similarly, the current value of your legal claim is not related to the legal fees you spent on it. This is one of the hardest truths for many people to accept. But think of it this way: imagine that you had another suit that was exactly the same claim, but instead of hiring the lawyers that you used, you'd hired other lawyers who did exactly the same things but charged half as much—or who charged twice as much. The strength of your claim is the same and its value going forward is the same, regardless of whether you were using cheap lawyers or expensive lawyers. The cost of going forward is far more important than the cost of having made it to where you are.

- "What do you estimate I'll receive if I win, or what do you estimate I'll have to pay if I lose?"
- "What do you estimate I will have to spend to get them to change their settlement position, and how much will this change be?" For instance, if another $15,000 is invested in attorney's fees, what more will be done, what is the likelihood of it changing the other side's position, and how much will that increase their settlement offer or decrease their demand?
- "Is this likely change in the other side's settlement position an appropriate return on the capital I invested (i.e., the additional legal fees) in terms of risk and in terms of the other uses to which I could have put this capital, such as new salespeople, advertising, or a better computer system?"

If you can keep your attention and energies focused on questions like these, and avoid the emotional pitfalls involved in litigation, you're sure to get a better net result.

Five

Managing Lawyers During Contract Negotiations

Every day, intelligent, astute, street-smart, and cautious business owners utter eight simple but sometimes very ill-advised words: *"Our lawyers can work out all the details."*

These people have no idea how dangerous that simple sentence can be. Their words imply that written contracts are merely a formality—no more difficult than pushing a button to have a computer spit out a form and then changing the names and dates, or dotting the i's and crossing the t's.

Their feeling is that since they and the other business owner trust each other and have reached a basic agreement on all of the "important" issues, the only task that remains is to put their deal down on paper. After all, isn't that what they pay the lawyers to do? To put everything that's been discussed into complicated legalese?

Business owners who think this way seldom want to read or re-read their lawyer's version of the written agreement—who wants to pore over all that legal mumbo jumbo when they already know what it is supposed to say? Sometimes they even tire of just talking about it. After all, they made a deal, and of course they are not about to go back on their word or renegotiate issues. All they want to do is sign the contract and then focus on what they do best and enjoy the most: making money. As far as they're concerned, the hard work is done; in a few weeks, after the lawyers have charged unconscionable amounts of money to translate their simple agreement into some incomprehensible legal language, they'll walk into a room, sign far too many copies of the contract, watch as it is witnessed by far too many people, and from that moment on, everything will be hunky-dory.

Unfortunately, what they sometimes find is that in a few weeks they are no closer to having a document to sign, and the lawyers are fighting with each other over issues involving things that the two business owners never considered. Not only are they now farther apart than they had thought, they have growing legal bills that are eating up ever more of their expected profits.

The clients invariably think, "First, let's kill all the lawyers." The lawyers invariably think, "God is in the details." The truth is that they both may be right. Yes, seemingly tiny, insignificant decisions are sometimes merely tiny and insignificant, and many lawyers cannot tell the difference. But, on occasion, seemingly insignificant decisions can make a world of difference. The fact is that many "legal issues" really have nothing to do with law. They're really business issues.

Consider this: if a serious dispute arises, how important is it to you that it be resolved in the court in your hometown or that of the other party? That might be insignificant if one party is in New York City and the other in northern New Jersey. But what if one is in New York and the other somewhere in Arizona?

Who should carry insurance? What should it cover? What should be the limit of the policies? Who bears the risk if the goods are damaged during delivery? Will the seller be responsible for the buyer's lost profits if delivery is delayed and the goods are not available for the Christmas selling season? What about the damage if a valued customer is forever lost due to a late delivery?

Rarely do business owners think to raise all these issues when they make a deal. Ask yourself: would you rather understand the consequences and then negotiate a resolution yourself, or not be bothered and simply let the lawyers decide?

Details of seemingly little import can have enormous business repercussions. A friend in the movie business told me that when George Lucas was negotiating with one of the large movie production companies about the original Star Wars film, the discussions were as long and painful as would be expected. The overriding questions had to do with ownership of the film that was going to be created and distribution of profits from its sale or licensing. What percentage should Lucas get for conceiving, writing, directing, and producing the film, and what percentage should the movie production company receive for taking the risk of putting up all the money for preproduction, production, shooting the film, making the prints, creating the TV commercials, buying the advertising media, and handling all of the administrative details? It has been widely rumored that after Lucas had been bullied, bruised, and threatened, eventually he accepted a division of ownership. He said he was reluctant to take the deal because he felt he had been coerced into accepting too little. And the production company people readily, and somewhat smugly, agreed. Money is power, and they felt justifiably pleased with the way in which they had wielded it.

Lucas then, it is told, made a request that seemed minor when compared with the "big" issues he had given in on. Would the production company—given that they had easily won the important game—grant him one concession? All he wanted was the merchandising rights, the right to license others to put the characters like Luke Skywalker on items like backpacks or notebooks. Until that time, all of the merchandising rights for all of the prior films ever made had been worth a combined total of about $10, so the immediate answer was, "Of course."

What happened next is history. The film made a fortune and the production company got a huge hunk of the pie. But the Star Wars merchandising made multiple fortunes—far, far more than the film itself.

It was a minor decision and, in all probability, one not likely to have been correctly evaluated by lawyers for either side. From a lawyer's point of view, it may have been nothing more than a relatively minor legal point—a topic that seemed unimportant. A lawyer might have never even thought of it.

Should you insist on being involved in everything? Of course not. But should you be easily accessible to discuss issues, opportunities, and even specific wording of contracts? Absolutely. And should you get frustrated with your lawyer for being farsighted enough to raise these issues and ask for your input? Never!

Some Do's of Negotiations

Over time, successful business owners have realized that a few basic practices can increase the efficiency and improve results of their negotiations and deal-making efforts.

Do negotiate with people who have the power to say yes.

In most companies, there are a lot of people who can say no and a lot more who will say, "I don't know, let me think about it." (It doesn't require a senior executive to halt or stall negotiations.) Real decision-makers have both the power and the courage to say yes. Talking with anyone else is often a waste of time—an interminably long, frustrating waste of time—that leads to higher attorneys' fees and longer negotiations in which something can go wrong.

This generally means that you should try to negotiate only with those people who have a substantial stake in the outcome. If you're negotiating with someone who isn't really vested in the outcome, you may not really be involved in a negotiation at all. Rather, you're simply having a long conversation with someone who has no real interest in taking the risks inherent in making a deal or even in ending the discussion.

Do meet face to face whenever possible.

There are lots of ways to negotiate. Negotiations can be done over the phone, via email, via fax, or by using intermediaries, hand signals, or carrier pigeons. Invariably, the best way is face to face.

Why? Because there is no place to hide when the negotiating principals are in the same room. You can tell if anyone is bored or not paying attention. Gamesmanship is kept to a minimum. Facial expressions provide important clues. Issues can be quickly and easily resolved. Decisions can be readily made. Both time and money are almost always saved.

Face-to-face discussions are not always necessary or possible. But when a deal is stalled, a face-to-face meeting is almost always the most efficient way to get it restarted.

Do use tact and diplomacy.

Unless you're doing it for a specific purpose, becoming angry or insulting isn't going to help. Displays of emotions like anger, impatience, boredom, or exasperation are currency that should be spent wisely.

Do know what's important to you and to them.

It is critical to know two things: the difference between what *you* want and what you need, and the difference between what *they* want and what they need. If, before you begin a negotiation, you know the difference between what you want and what you need, you will make wiser decisions. Rarely can you get everything you ask for; in other words, there are times you will have to compromise on some issues. In considering those compromises, you will do best when you stay focused on the things you think are really important—the things you *need*—and prevail on those. At that point it's much easier to know when to make concessions on issues that you merely *want,* since those things are not as important to you. Don't get confused and blow a deal even though you got everything you needed but not everything you wanted. Just as importantly, don't give up something you need for something you only want.

For example, because of advances in technology, a retailer's ability to put antennae on the roof of its store in a shopping center has become very important. My partner worked on a lease for a client renting out space in a shopping center that involved two outstanding issues: the rate of interest that would accrue to unpaid rent in the event of a tenant's default, and the scope of the tenant's liability if the roof antenna it needed to erect were to fall or be blown over. In my mind, these were simple to resolve. Since the tenant was putting up the antenna, the tenant should pay for any damages if it fell. But more importantly, if the antenna fell, the damage could be huge—holes in the roof, damage to the nearby air conditioning condenser, injury to a customer on the sidewalk, or publicity that would scare away customers or potential tenants. I felt this client needed protection against all of these kinds of damages. But with regard to the interest rate on unpaid rent, this was something we wanted, but probably would never need; after all, if there were large amounts of unpaid rent, the tenant would very likely be out of business, and if so, it would probably have no assets with which to pay the unpaid rent or the high interest.

Similarly, when making the decision to say no and run the risk of losing a potentially profitable deal, it helps to know whether you are saying no to something the other side needs or simply wants. If it is something they want, you will be risking far less and can probably wait out their unhappiness. But if it is something they need, your saying no should be carefully considered since it has a high risk of blowing the deal.

Some Don'ts of Negotiations.

In addition to knowing the things to do, you should also be aware of those things you want to avoid.

Don't waste time negotiating with anyone who isn't a decision-maker.

Two representatives, regardless of their competence, intelligence, or best intentions, sometimes keep negotiating forever because they do not have the power to concede a point their boss wants, or to walk away from the deal because they could not get what their boss needs. Reason, logic, and business realities won't help reach a rational compromise because the real decision-maker, the one to be reasoned with, is not in the room.

Even worse, there are times when you leave thinking you've made a deal and are finally done talking, only to discover a few days later through a meek phone call or a letter from the other party's lawyer that their boss still has more to be discussed. So, essentially, you've wasted your own time and, if your attorney was with you, you've wasted a considerable amount of money as well.

Don't negotiate with anyone who doesn't know when to give in.

There are few things as destructive to negotiations as someone who continues to argue over issues that are of little or no business importance. In the end, nothing of consequence is accomplished while time and money are wasted. These are people who will simply not give in.

When you have to negotiate with this type of person, sometimes the only wise behavior is to simply say no and walk away. Any attempt to continue to talk or reason is not only a waste of time and energy, but also an opportunity for you to be worn down by the other person's stubbornness.

Don't negotiate with people who make it clear they'll leave nothing on the table.

Negotiations should not be competitions. They do not always require a winner or a loser on absolutely every point. In fact, many successful business owners understand that negotiations that result in mutual satisfaction are the first step in building trusting business relationships—and that trust can be very valuable when you need to resolve the problems that inevitably crop up. The willingness to give the other side something they want, in addition to what they need, can be an investment in building that sort of trust.

On the other hand, the wisdom of doing business with people who will leave nothing on the table is always questionable. After all, you are learning during the negotiation that if a problem arises later, these people will exert every bit of economic leverage they have to win that dispute as well. A deal may promise profit, but almost all deals also hold some subtle but real risks, especially if the other people involved have a win-lose perspective.

Don't negotiate with someone who is antagonistic.

Negotiations proceed best in a relationship of trust. Anyone who is insensitive or unaware of the importance of diplomacy and tact throughout the discussions will almost certainly turn out to be an obstacle when it comes to finding win-win solutions. And it is often true that an antagonistic, tactless business owner will choose an antagonistic, tactless lawyer with whom you will also have to deal.

Don't negotiate with someone who insists on only using the phone.

You can't judge a person's anxiety, enthusiasm, or body language over the phone. Of course, there are times when the telephone is fine, but for the major discussions, you don't want to be dealing with someone who will not meet face to face.

Don't negotiate with someone who has no financial incentive to make the deal.

In other words, don't negotiate with someone who is being paid by the hour or for whom making the deal is riskier than walking away. Both conditions are often the case for consultants. The longer the discussions take, the happier they are. And there is no reason to believe that long negotiations will help you reach a more favorable conclusion. The only thing certain about long negotiations is that they will cost you more money. And often, the longer the negotiations, the better the consultants look. On the other hand, some are in a position where not making a deal is in their best interest. After all, they will often be blamed if a deal they made goes badly, but given no credit if it works out.

Don't talk about what you won't concede.

Negotiating most often takes place by talking. The fact that you are talking about something indicates that you are still negotiating about it. If a subject is not open for negotiation, do not talk about it. Make your actions consistent with your statements. Do not try to justify why the subject is closed—just state that the subject is not to be talked about and act accordingly.

On the other hand, if the other side says something is non-negotiable, but they are willing to keep talking about it, this may mean that you can get them to change their position. Sometimes, subjects that may not seem open for negotiation may be compromised without sacrificing what either you or they need. Remember, though: talking about why the subject is nonnegotiable, even when it's done to justify your position, is a negotiation.

Don't be afraid to walk away.

A very smart client of mine once observed, "Sometimes nothing is as powerful as walking away." There are times when merely saying no is not enough, where the most effective and sometimes the only way to be understood is to physically remove yourself from the discussion. This does not mean that the discussion is over. On the contrary, my experience has been that in at least 75 percent of the situations in which one party has physically walked away, the negotiations have continued. Walking away shows that the party who is saying no really means it. It's also true that a party who says no and continues to talk really means maybe.

"But," you might ask, "what do I do if I am forced to do business with someone who won't meet in person, who is antagonistic, or who waffles about decisions?"

The answer is to be careful and to adopt a strategy or mode of behavior designed to deal with the problem that wastes as little time as possible. For instance, tell hostile parties that you won't talk with them unless they act more politely. Ask them why they are so angry—maybe their anger will abate, and even if it doesn't, you might learn how to address or sidestep it. Go to meetings at their office. State your position clearly and then refuse to discuss it. Insist on talking with their boss. Remember, there is something they want from you, otherwise they would not be talking with you. Figure out what that is and be clear about what you need in return.

Good Lawyers Can Help

As you go through the lengthy process of negotiating, your lawyer can—and should—provide valuable input about those things that your lawyer can do better than you. For instance:

- Good lawyers learn through experience to identify business relationships that have a high risk of creating problems. It's your decision to make, but your lawyer ought to pinpoint potential problems. Many people have dealt with a contractor who does a wonderful job of remodeling their house or adding a new den. Sometimes after this type of experience, the homeowner and the contractor might conclude that they can make money together by buying and then remodeling old houses. They strike an agreement whereby the contractor will find the house and do all the work at his cost, the happy homeowner will provide the necessary cash to buy the house and the raw materials, and the profits will be divided equally. Although there are exceptions, this arrangement rarely works. When push comes to shove, the contractor will almost always do the work on his other projects first. After all, the profits on those projects go directly to the contractor's pocket, while the contractor only gets to keep 50 percent of the profits on the remodeling project. Money on these other projects may get paid monthly and can be used to buy groceries and satisfy other immediate needs, while the 50 percent payoff from the remodeled house would not be seen until the work is completed and the house is sold. That is probably many months away. These economic realities tend to create a business relationship that has a high likelihood of becoming dysfunctional.
- Good lawyers help determine which ambiguities in contracts can be ignored and which can cause trouble. Gray areas in written agreements are difficult to enforce.

Yet not all contract provisions need to be totally clear; some contract ambiguities can work to your advantage. Others may threaten the whole purpose of the contract. For example, if you are the buyer of a complicated custom-built machine, you may find it helpful if the contract is ambiguous about whether you must pay when the machine starts operating, or after a period of testing and training. On the other hand, if the contract is even slightly ambiguous about what the machine is supposed to do, you risk paying a premium price for a machine that doesn't operate as you had expected.

- Good lawyers should be objective and able to see win-win solutions to problems that others may miss. In many negotiations you may be so financially or emotionally involved that it is often quite difficult for you to be objective. Your focus, rightfully, is on protecting yourself from risk while not losing the opportunity to make money. Good lawyers should add value in two distinct ways. First, their objectivity may assist everyone in discovering issues that can be conceded—often at no cost—that make both sides more comfortable. And second, they should be able to stop you from making compromises that seem attractive at the time but could increase your risk. Good lawyers who find solutions that benefit (or are, at least, acceptable to) both sides create a very positive atmosphere that could lead to more constructive resolution of future difficulties. There are often win-win solutions—even in some otherwise bitter disputes—if only someone has the objectivity to see them and the courage to suggest them.

- Good lawyers act as a diplomatic buffer. In the role of a go-between, they can ask direct (and often blunt) questions that, if asked by you, might destroy the relationship you are trying to develop. For you to be the good cop, someone else needs to be the bad cop. Lawyers, for obvious reasons, make excellent bad cops and allow you to be aggressive and confrontational without ruining your relationship with the person with whom you hope to have long-term business involvement.

- Good lawyers act as your scapegoat. If you want to change your mind, delay, or speed up the transaction; expand the scope of the discussions; or renegotiate critical terms, you can use your lawyer as an excuse. How many times do you hear people say, "I hate to bring this up, but my lawyer says that we should..."? You should always have a lawyer with shoulders broad enough to carry the burden of being blamed even when you are the cause.

You Need to Be a Good Manager

Even if you have hired the best lawyer in the world, or at least in your neighborhood, and even if you follow all the do's and don'ts of good negotiating, your attention and involvement are still very important. Ultimately, lawyers are suppliers, and like all suppliers, they make mistakes that can be avoided if you exercise effective management.

Good management is not limited to reading every word of a contract, although that is almost always a good idea. In a paradoxical way, good management is both easier and harder than that.

Don't let the lawyers spend time on unimportant issues.

The key word here is "unimportant." If the discussion is valuable in terms of finding out the other side's goals so that you can reach win-win solutions, then by all means spend all the time that's necessary. But long discussions that are no more than philosophical musings on why each side is right are just potentially deal-killing chances for the lawyers to show off their cleverness. Likewise, it is in no one's best interest to get bogged down on issues of little consequence.

Prevent the lawyers from generating ill will, especially over unimportant issues.

The problem with fights, or even heated discussions, about unimportant issues isn't just that they cost you extra legal fees (though they certainly will). The potential consequences are much greater. The more emotional heat that gets built up, the less chance there is for trust to develop between you and the other side. Even worse, these heated discussions create delays that may result in the other side getting a better deal elsewhere or changing its mind. If this happens, look in the mirror before you blame the lawyers. Conscientious lawyers believe that they are pursuing an issue on your behalf. They often pursue your goals like pit bulls that won't let go unless they're called off. And when the issue is important, this is exactly how you want them to be.

But it's your money that's being spent and your business that's being affected. Ultimately, it's up to you to decide which contractual issues are important enough to discuss and which are just a waste of time. After all, your lawyer will never know as much about your business as you do, and his or her well-meaning evaluation of a risk may simply be uninformed.

Make sure that the tone of the negotiations remains appropriate.

If you decide that an adversarial tone during a negotiation is appropriate, that's fine. Your lawyers should be as aggressive as you want them to be. But, if you'd rather there be a tone of mutual respect, you should make that clear to your lawyer. Don't let your lawyer make enemies for you without your permission. This is something you can and should control.

Make sure that the other side's body language, demeanor, and tone of voice are closely observed.

In every transaction, there are critical issues or *deal points*. When these points are being negotiated, someone should take careful note of the other party's behavior. Were the other principals nervous, sweating, distracted, or afraid to look anyone in the eye? In other words, when they said no on a critical issue, was it genuine or a bluff?

If you are engaged in the discussion to the extent that you cannot make these evaluations, you need to have a lawyer who has the skill and experience to do this. Needless concession can sometimes be avoided if someone is paying enough attention to the nonverbal communication.

Words Can Hurt

The language used in a contract can often have a very real and harmful effect on the feelings of the people reading it. Words have enormous power, even when those words are used in a business contract.

Business owners (especially when negotiating with a family member) should make sure that their lawyers write documents that are not demeaning or insulting. There is no reason to raise the emotional stakes with a poor or thoughtless choice of language. A lawyer who can only write in stilted, hard-to-understand, and demeaning language is rarely a good lawyer.

If a father is chairman of the board and his son is president of the company, the son's employment contract can have the same legal meaning while having dramatically different emotional meanings. One lawyer might write:

Junior must get the approval of his father before he decides to sell the company, issue new stock, refinance the company's debt, or make expenditures of more than the amount set out in an annual budget, which his father must approve each year.

Another, more tactful lawyer might say the same thing by writing:

Decisions with regard to the sale of the company, the issuance of new stock, the refinancing of the company's debt, or expenditures of more than the annual budget shall be made unanimously by the president and chairman of the board.

Some lawyers have not been taught to consider the emotional reactions of the people who read the contracts that they write. But while many good lawyers sometimes read and write contracts without regard for their emotional tone of voice, it doesn't automatically make them bad lawyers or bad people. Rather, it just means that it's your responsibility to keep your lawyers on track. You must clearly explain the type of legal service that you require—even if it means your lawyers must change how they write.

In addition to the choice of language, choice of content also has potential emotional consequences. Certain kinds of contracts, by their very nature, are sure to raise hackles.

A lawyer may suggest that in the best interests of a company, all of its personnel should sign noncompete agreements. That's what many would consider good, conservative, cautious advice. But hidden in that course of action is a series of risks that result from the emotional consequences of making that request. Who can doubt that the mere act of asking sons or daughters to sign a noncompete agreement could give them the impression that their parent doesn't trust them and that they should reconsider whether to reciprocate that trust? Emotions are likely to run high, even if the doubt, hurt, and lack of trust is kept hidden for a while. This seemingly neutral act, which the lawyer thought was prudent, can corrode the type of healthy relationships that are so important to a successful business.

That lawyer does have a point. But business owners are responsible for telling their lawyer, "This is something that is too insulting for me to impose on my child. The risk that results from that insult is greater than the risk you are trying to protect me against." If that's how you feel, that's what you should say. Your job as a business owner and a client requires that you make the final decisions. Not having that contract may turn out to have been a mistake, but at least it would be a mistake that you made, not a mistake that was made because you did not properly supervise your lawyers' work.

Negotiations Are Educational

If you think the only purposes of contract negotiations are to get as good a deal as possible and to craft a bulletproof contract, you're missing a golden opportunity to learn crucial information about the other side. I have often noted that what my clients learn about the other side during contract negotiations is sometimes more important than the contract itself. The insights that you can obtain during negotiations—about the character, morals, and values of the people with whom you are about to do business—can be hugely significant.

Certainly, the written contract is of enormous importance. But, no matter how well written a document may be, disputes over the language can still occur. There are two reasons why this is so:

1. The English language is often easy to misunderstand.
2. Someone can make or save a lot of money by figuring out how to misunderstand it. This is especially true when someone hires a bright, intelligent, and highly motivated lawyer for the sole purpose of finding any possible ambiguity in the contract's language.

Some people are honest, prompt, trustworthy, open, and willing to be fair. Others are rigid, dishonest about their goals, deceptive about their motives, and unwilling to compromise or accommodate your needs. By paying close attention to the other party's behavior during negotiations, you can develop a strong sense of their trustworthiness and rationality.

The most common causes of problems are the contingencies that no one was able to foresee. At one time earlier in my career, I met another lawyer and we eventually decided to start our own law firm. We both trusted each other enough to believe that if we were successful, we would not want to end our relationship, and we would have no trouble working out a solution to any problems. But, we were old enough to know that if we were not successful and wanted to end our relationship, neither of us wanted the other to be in a position to exert economic leverage to extract an unfair concession. So we decided that the one issue we would agree on in advance was how we would break up the firm if either of us so desired. My partner's concern was that I not be in a position to take away the office suite and staff that he had already put in place. My concern was that he not be able to kick me out so abruptly that I could not find new offices to keep my legal practice functioning. We negotiated a resolution that very fairly fulfilled our respective needs.

As fate would have it, something happened that neither of us would have ever anticipated. My partner received an offer to become the general counsel of his largest client—literally, a career-changing opportunity. Although we had carefully negotiated break-up provisions based on what we both anticipated—he would stay and I would leave—we had not thought it possible that my partner would want to leave and I would want to stay.

Fortunately, the story had a happy ending. We were able to accommodate each other's needs with no friction and, in his new job, my partner became my largest client and has remained one of my closest friends. But the lesson remains the same: unforeseen events can and will happen with regularity. That's why smart business owners all reach the same conclusion about how to fully protect themselves against unforeseen events. They realize that whenever possible, they should do business with people who will resolve problems rationally and in an atmosphere of mutual trust.

How do you find those people? You pay attention—very close attention—to the way they handle themselves during negotiations. You see not only what decisions they make, but also the way the go about making those decisions. You study and evaluate their thought process, their commitment to fairness, and their tolerance for hearing other points of view and accommodating other people's needs.

The best-written contract usually cannot protect against the other side's basic dishonesty. When promises are broken, business owners are often frustrated by the difficulty and expense of enforcing even the most carefully drafted contracts. That's understandable. Fighting a lawsuit is almost always a frustrating experience and one that is often quite wasteful.

But, bemoaning the inefficiency of the legal system will not change reality. If promises are violated, you will almost never make as much money as if they are honored. The key to success is to do business with people whom you trust to honor their promises. It really is that simple.

Act Like the Boss

Remember the situation of the business owner who needed to fire the company's elderly employee? Well, that is a perfect example of the role in which business owners typically find themselves. A decision must be made between two imperfect alternatives. One is to keep an underperforming employee on the job for an extended period of time, thus threatening the work ethic and morale of the remaining employees. The other is to fire that employee, who may then bring a lawsuit that could cost tens of thousands of dollars.

If you are a business owner, you need to remember that it is your company, your life, and your income that will be affected by the decision. The decision is yours to make. Letting the lawyer make the decision is simply wrong.

Several years ago, when the Chicago Bulls were in the midst of their sixth championship season, I was at a game against the New York Knicks. The Bulls were trailing by one point with three seconds left on the clock. The ball was in the hands of the Bull's Scottie Pippen, an indisputable all-star. After he dribbled to somewhere above the free-throw circle, he found himself open for a shot—but passed the ball to Michael Jordan. With one second on the clock, Jordan made the shot that won the game.

Driving home, I turned on the radio just in time to hear a live interview with Scottie Pippen. When asked why he passed the ball to Michael Jordan and didn't take the shot himself, Pippen simply said, "That's why he gets paid the big bucks."

Just as this is true in professional sports, so too is it true in business. The owner gets the big bucks because he, and not his lawyer, has the will and desire to make the critical decisions.

▶ *Six*

Ten Great Ways to Get More
from Your Lawyer for Less: A Review

To this point of the book, I've covered a breadth of different aspects of the business owner's relationship with lawyers. Let me go over some of those key ideas again, with a particular focus on the one aspect that should be of most interest to you—getting the best legal service at the best value.

1. When It Comes to Risk, Get Your Lawyer to Give Real Advice

Business requires taking risks; managing these risks successfully is what increases profits. If a client asks whether she has a claim against a supplier whose parts malfunctioned, good lawyers should realize that this is a complicated question, and they might not know the answer off the top of their heads. But they should also realize that it is of no value to do research and then write a long memo that discusses in detail the cases and the law, and then conclude, "Well, we cannot say for sure that you will win, and thus this will be a risk." Stating that is simply stating the obvious; it has no value as advice. A more helpful memo, one worth paying for, might conclude, "Although there is no guarantee, we think that you have a 70 percent chance of success. The lawsuit will require an investment of about $75,000 in legal fees if there is a trial. In view of the potential recovery of $300,000 and the fact that your only alternative at this point in time is to drop the matter entirely, filing a lawsuit seems like a prudent course of action.

Our expectation would be that a settlement offer in the range of $100,000 can be reasonably expected after about $20,000 of legal fees has been expended. Once we reach the point of filing the lawsuit and doing the initial work, we can reassess the wisdom and cost of further proceedings." Ultimately, you are your lawyer's boss. Don't accept or pay for advice that does not help you make choices between meaningful alternatives and actions. You should insist on receiving honest and creative cost-benefit analysis. If you have no alternatives, you do not need to pay a lawyer to tell you that your only possible course of action is imperfect.

2. Don't Be Fooled by Fantasy Lawyering

As a business owner, you must be realistic about what to expect from a lawyer. The most common fantasy is that there are lawyers who, like Wild West gunslingers, stroll into the court room and scare everyone into doing what you want. The reality is that courtroom fighting is almost always a lose-lose proposition (for the clients, at least—the lawyers can make plenty of money in this situation). Another equally appealing but misleading fantasy is that a lawyer can be the stalwart protector of your rights. This usually means shielding you from risk, guaranteeing that others will recognize and respect your rights (real and assumed), and serving as a bulletproof shield against adversity. Lawyers who foster these kinds of fantasies often negatively affect your profits. In reality, you should hire lawyers who do a good job of outlining your risks, providing you with alternatives, and letting you do your job: to make decisions among different business alternatives, all of which have different risks.

3. It's Not All About Justice

Justice is a very ephemeral concept. Ultimately, our legal system defines "justice" as the process of having an independent judge or jury resolve a dispute without bias by consistently applying the same rules to everyone. That does *not* mean that they will do their job without mistakes; in fact, lots of mistakes are made. It also does *not* mean that you will win. If there is one thing that justice is *not*, it is not a system where you always win. This is a hard pill for many people to swallow. After all, on television and in movies, litigation is exciting drama where you know who is good and who is bad and "justice" prevails because right inevitably wins out over wrong.

In reality, litigation, or any other means of dispute resolution, is simply dispute resolution—a means to resolve conflicting claims. Any system that resolves disputes, like any other system developed by or known to human beings, is imperfect. Revenge, vindication, or proving you are "right" are goals the legal system is not designed or equipped to efficiently or effectively accommodate. The *only* rational goal for someone involved in business litigation should be to make as much or lose as little money as possible. A lawyer who encourages you to believe that litigation will bring you emotional or moral vindication (which is what most people think of as "justice") will drain you of more of your resources and time than you can probably afford.

4. If You Want to See Cheerleaders, Go to a Basketball Game

Your lawyers are your consultants. As such, they must provide you with brutally honest advice—that's what you deserve. Yet many clients may encourage their lawyers to be less than candid by showing disappointment or anger when a lawyer says something they do not want to hear. Smart lawyers learn to recognize these clients a mile away; as a result, some become cheerleaders who simply tell these clients what they want to hear. To avoid turning your lawyer into a cheerleader, be sure not to punish him for suggesting that your notions of how a dispute should be resolved are wrong, or for honestly advising you that the result of your actions might not be in your best interest.

5. Avoid Small Lawyers, Not Small Law Firms

A surprisingly large number of people are overly impressed by lawyers who appear to be very successful. A big office, some flashy awards on the wall, lots of partners, and some strategic name-dropping of important clients can go a long way toward persuading some people that a lawyer must be very good. After all, how else could they have gotten an office on a high floor with such a nice view? And, those same people are sometimes so flattered that these corner-office lawyers will take their comparatively trivial case that they forgive the lawyer for inattention or for assigning them an inexperienced assistant. After all, they think, they are not important enough to engage the interest of such a successful person and if they complain, they will be fired as clients. It was in this context that someone once observed, "There are no small matters, only small lawyers." A small matter to some big-shot lawyer, who is used to working for an international conglomerate that can afford to pay Cadillac prices, can be a very big matter to you, and you should not be embarrassed by that fact. If your matter is going to be handled by a small lawyer—a big-shot who will ignore it, or pass it off to a junior attorney with no practical experience—you run the risk of being very poorly served. The fact that your small lawyer is in a big law firm that handles big matters will not do you any good. Good lawyers are found in all sorts of settings—in small towns and big cities, in small and large law firms. The trick is not to find a big law firm with small lawyers. Anyone with enough money can do that. The trick is to find the big lawyers, be they in small or large firms.

6. Your Lawyer Should Make Sense, Not War

Most people get angry in the course of a dispute. And when people are angry, they want revenge. However, as angry as you might be, it is almost always a mistake to hire lawyers whose primary skill is the ability to be insulting, dismissive, or demeaning. Or lawyers who suggest that they are so tough that the people who made you angry will wither in fear.

No matter how angry the participants, disputes are most efficiently solved through compromise. From your point of view, of course, it's the *other* parties that should make the major compromises. Being realistic and rational (which sometimes lets you *pretend* to be unrealistic or irrational) is always best. Insulting others, even if only through body language or demeaning statements, may be emotionally satisfying, but it usually accomplishes nothing other than making it harder for them to agree to make the compromises that will benefit you. Regardless of how other people might act, your lawyer should first and foremost make sense and not blindly make war. Watching your lawyer be insulting or demeaning may make you feel good, but you are usually making a mistake if you encourage, or tolerate, that behavior, since it almost never does anything more than increase the attorneys' fees and make the dispute harder to resolve.

7. Consider Negotiations a Test of Character

Many business owners think that the goal of a contract negotiation is to get the best possible deal and a bulletproof contract. But few contracts are bulletproof. An overlooked value of negotiations is that they allow you to test the character of the other parties before you are bound to do business with them. You have a terrific opportunity to judge both their integrity and how they will react if problems arise. During the negotiating stage, you and your lawyers can observe whether this person looks for fair win-win solutions or thinks only of win-lose outcomes. People who take the time to understand and respect each other's needs and concerns are more likely to make fair concessions when unforeseen problems arise. Your lawyers should be able to give you a good evaluation of these qualities as part of their service to you.

8. Don't Be Intimidated—Lawyers Are Consultants, Not Wizards

Lawyers are not infallible and their skills do not involve magic. You can and should understand what they do on your behalf and why. It is your responsibility to supervise and understand your lawyers' work. It is your lawyers' responsibility to make their work intelligible to you and to your staff.

9. Pay Less for the Same—Encourage Competition

Encouraging competition is usually a good way to get good service for less money, even among lawyers. There is no reason why all of your legal work needs to be done by one lawyer or one law firm. Having your lawyers mindful of the fact that they are being compared to others is almost always in your best interests.

10. Reward Efficiency and Honesty

Reward your lawyer by trying to work out fee arrangements that promote an open relationship, and give your lawyers incentives to give you the type of honest advice you should be seeking. Avoid fee arrangements that reward the lawyer for advising you to take more or fewer risks than you would intend. For instance, if you want a lawyer to help you protect yourself from unanticipated risks in buying a business or a piece of real estate, it is a mistake to motivate the lawyer to ignore risk by promising a bonus merely if the deal closes.

◆ PART II

Family Business Issues

Seven

The Family Business

A significant number of privately owned businesses, especially smaller and mid-sized businesses, are owned by families. Because of the emotional issues involved in family relationships, the complexities involved in running a family-owned business—especially dealing with any conflict among the family members—can be very difficult and painful. Moreover, the challenges involved in dealing with problems among family member "owners" who also work as company employees are also fairly singular—as are the issues involved in being a nonfamily member involved in running or partially owning a family-owned company. When these family relationships are not functioning smoothly, the difficulty of finding solutions can be unimaginable.

Because these problems and their solutions are so unique, I felt they merited their own section of this book.

Business owners can have blind spots for many different things, but dealing with family business relationships is one of the biggest and most problematic blind spots I've had to deal with in my forty years of legal experience. Rational, business-like decision-making can go out the window when family conflict is involved.

The Value of Business Advisors

During the last twenty years, there has been a healthy increase in the number of highly trained consultants who have developed the skills necessary to help resolve the problems of a family that owns a business. These family business advisors, much like therapists, bring a deep understanding of the nature and depth of the feelings that each family member can have toward parents, children, cousins, siblings, etc. With this understanding, these advisors can evaluate how these feelings might inhibit rational decision-making and how to help the family members make decisions that deal with both the emotional family issues and also with the complex business challenges.

Certainly, great value can be obtained by the family having an advisor who can privately talk with the various family members affected by a decision to gather information with the promise that it will remain confidential. Under these circumstances, both information and feelings will be disclosed that the company and its family owners would not want to become public—issues like drug abuse, sexual behavior, sibling jealousies, overbearing parents, adults acting like rebellious teenagers, or potentially improper income tax payments.

It is fully appropriate for family business advisors to make these promises regarding confidentiality, and for family members to trust that sensitive information will not be conveyed to other family members or to competitors. A son who confides his feeling that his mother is interfering with rational business decisions should not find himself quoted to his mother without his permission. Similarly, criticisms of a family member by a nonfamily executive should not be disclosed to that family member if he or she is the type of person who might precipitously fire the nonfamily executive out of spite. Disclosures made by a brother should be held secret from another brother if they could potentially destroy the relationship.

Unfortunately, there is a hidden risk in the use of an advisor such as this. If a lawsuit should ever be initiated between these parties, these communications are not *legally* confidential. Lawyers, doctors, and priests have what is referred to as an *absolute privilege*. That means that except under the most unusual of circumstances, courts will not require them to disclose information obtained in confidential communications. Non-physician therapists and accountants sometimes have a more limited privilege, which varies from state to state. However, a lawyer, accountant, or therapist who acts in the role of family business advisor—providing something other than the express legal, medical, spiritual, or accounting advice of his or her accreditation—may not have *any* privilege.

In other words, both business owners and family business advisors should be careful when dealing with a situation where a lawsuit seems likely. Consultants may promise the people they talk with that their communications will be kept confidential, but, if brought to a judge, they might be ordered to testify about the content of that communication.

Problems with a Family Member Owner/Employee

When a business fires someone, it usually finds itself with an angry ex-employee who has only the normal rights regarding breach of contract or discrimination. Dealing with these rights is complicated—but not nearly as complicated as when the employee is a family member who also owns a part of the company. When a business fires an employee who is also an owner, it finds itself not only with an angry ex-employee (with whom the owner may still have to share future Thanksgiving or Christmas dinners), but also with an angry shareholder—someone who has been on the inside of the business's financial dealings and knows if there are any tensions or secrets in the family that could cause *very* serious problems.

In the few family-owned businesses that are very large, angry family shareholders rarely cause problems. For example, family shareholders of a business with publicly traded stock can sell their stock at a fair market value and thus have little business motive to cause problems. Similarly, a fired employee-shareholder in a third- or fourth-generation family business with dividend-paying stock that is widely owned by both employed and nonemployed family—or in a business that has a well-established liquidity program that purchases stock at a fair market value—will probably do no more than sell the stock and avoid family functions. But no law of nature dictates that there will be peace even under these circumstances. At least once a year, it seems, we can read about a fired employee-shareholder of a very successful family business who has struck out on a course of action that is interesting enough to deserve a story on the front page of *The Wall Street Journal*.

The reality is that in many smaller family businesses, one of the major advantages of stock ownership is the chance to go to work each morning, or to have your children hold guaranteed jobs. Even though the presidents of those businesses may have the legal right to fire any employee—even employees who are shareholders or whose parents are shareholders—the likely cost of that firing (once the ex-employee finds a clever lawyer) will be the purchase of the minority interest at a price higher than market value.

From an employment-law point of view, as long as the reasons for termination are performance-based and can be established either through witnesses or documents, there is no significant difference between firing an owner-employee and firing a nonowner-employee. The legal case is further strengthened if the company made the firing decision with input or approval from an independent board of directors or even an independent board of advisors.

But owner-employees can mount an attack on another front because of their legal standing (as an owner) and insider knowledge (as a family member privy to any secrets the management may have). For example, an owner can claim that other owners are breaching their fiduciary duty by reimbursing themselves for questionable expense-account claims, by not working when they're supposed to be working, by using company funds to remodel their houses, by paying themselves excessive salaries, or any number of other activities that are legally questionable but common in small businesses. The combination of that legal standing and those secrets can make it very uncomfortable for owners to refuse to buy out the ex-employee's stock at a premium. Those owners should be prepared to confront the choice of either buying back stock or having the company's working capital sapped by the legal fees required for what may at first seem like a frivolous lawsuit, but will, nevertheless, be expensive and time-consuming to defend.

Thus, firing family shareholders will typically result in negotiations to buy their stock. Since their ability to cause trouble greatly exceeds the value of the stock in the marketplace (a minority interest in a small company that pays no dividends and is controlled by the chief employee usually has no market value), the controlling shareholders should be prepared to pay far more than they think the fired employees' stock is worth.

Why Buy Out a Shareholder with No Right to Be Bought Out?

"But," you might say, "I thought of this in advance and asked our lawyer whether the cousin I was about to fire had the right to force us to buy out her stock. Our lawyer said, 'Absolutely no such right exists.' Are you telling me my lawyer is wrong?"

No, what that lawyer said is true. Unfortunately, you asked the wrong questions, and, being very literal, the lawyer answered what you asked, but did not necessarily tell you what you needed to know.

When the person being fired knows that a particular company's closet hides a skeleton, the refusal to purchase that shareholder's stock (and with it their silence) leaves her with no option but to try to get that skeleton to march across a courtroom as soon as possible.

"But," you might point out, "years ago I wanted to sue someone and my lawyer taught me that courtrooms are not just there for anyone to whine to the judge. You have to have a case, a cause of action, or a claim for relief. Otherwise the judge may impose sanctions against you."

That is also true. So then how can a minority shareholder bring a suit to force a buyout? In many ways. For example, most states have a legal framework that allows a minority shareholder both to question the fairness of the officers' salaries and to cause the sale of a company that is abusing its shareholders or breaking laws. "Abuse" is rarely clearly defined, thus giving judges broad discretion to correct perceived unfairness. Judges often think there is a premium on resolving disputes among family members, and often do not think that there should be a financial premium placed on having majority control of a small family business. Thus, when a judge hints that "abuse" could be defined as not providing any cash benefits for the nonemployed minority shareholders, a purchase of the stock at above-market value becomes an appealing compromise.

In addition, knowledge of some common business practices often provides the leverage necessary to force a buyout. Some businesses cut corners, particularly in relation to taxes and salaries. A client of mine once observed, "What's the fun of having your own business if you can't cheat a little on taxes?" Now, very few family business owners think of themselves as tax cheats. Yet when their accounting methods are looked at in the stark, cold focus of a cross-examination, it may look like cheating is exactly what they are doing. Putting personal family travel or dinners on your expense account, having the business pay for personal cell phones for the owners' kids or spouses, keeping company computers at home for use by kids or spouses, or using the company credit card to purchase tickets to sporting events that no customer attends—none of these are unheard-of practices. Of course, when these perks are spread around to all the family members, no one has incentive to complain. But when these perks are passed out in a preferential manner, with nonemployed family members receiving nothing, hard feelings quickly develop.

Similarly, in many family businesses, the payment of excess cash to shareholders as salaries has a distinct tax advantage over the declaration of dividends. When money is paid out as a salary, it is only taxed to the recipient. When money is paid out as a dividend, it is first taxed at the corporate level and then is again taxed to the recipient. Privately held companies rarely pay dividends for exactly this reason. Questionable salaries get paid in numerous ways. The daughter who is a full-time college student might be paid her allowance as a salary even though she never comes to work. Having the money taxed in her low tax bracket, as opposed to her father's high tax bracket, has obvious financial advantages. Or a widowed mother might be paid a salary equal to her husband's as a way of providing her regular income, even though her contribution to the company is minimal. Family directors might be paid handsome fees and travel expenses for going to quarterly board of directors meetings in exotic places.

These practices have legal implications when looked at by shareholders who want out. Officers, directors, and shareholders who approve questionable salaries also risk being accused of breaching their duties to the minority shareholders. It doesn't take Clarence Darrow to see this vulnerability as a tool for encouraging the buy-back of the fired shareholder's stock.

So, what does this mean? That firing an underperforming shareholder-employee is never possible? No, of course not. Firing an underperforming shareholder-employee is not only possible, but it is often essential for the business to survive. However, it must be done with the knowledge that the fired shareholder will probably want to be bought out, and that you must make realistic plans to meet that desire.

Dealing with Unhappy Shareholders— The Virtues of Liquidity Agreements

Obviously, it can be disastrous to have unhappy shareholders involved in a business against their will. If their investment in the business is a material part of their net worth, the absence of a fair way out will lead to dysfunctional relationships, if not lawsuits. Drafting an agreement that gives shareholders an exit strategy is one of the more valuable things a lawyer can provide to a family business. Yet, few privately owned or family businesses have a means to get disgruntled minority shareholders to sell their stock at a fair price.

Surprisingly, such agreements are either unknown to many lawyers or rarely requested by business owners. Why is this surprising? Because business owners wise enough to adopt such agreements dramatically lower the potential for mistrust and frustration by the minority shareholders who are not employed, while increasing the opportunity to adopt previously unavailable long-term business strategies that contribute to profitability. These *liquidity agreements* hold great promise for keeping a family business peaceful and profitable.

In these sorts of agreements, the stock price is set by a formula that is regularly adjusted to reflect profitability, the value of comparable companies in the same industry, and an appropriate minority discount. For example, a plumbing supplies company might adopt a formula that values the company at the same price-earnings ratio that the market places on the stock of a publicly traded competitor, requires the recalculation of that price every six months, and imposes a 10 percent minority discount. The majority/controlling shareholders would not take advantage of this option, because they could always sell the company and not have to incur the minority discount. On the other hand, this provides minority shareholders a way to liquidate their investment and diversify their portfolio if they are unhappy with the performance of the company or are not confident with the majority's stewardship of the company's future.

These agreements can also obligate the company to buy the stock on a first come, first served basis, with this obligation limited to a preset percentage of the stock each year. This type of agreement has significant benefits:

- It does away with much of the need to pressure younger shareholders into signing prenuptial agreements when they get married. Most judges and lawyers would agree that it is extremely unlikely that a value put on the stock in this way (long before the marriage was entered into) could be successfully challenged during a divorce. The typical goals of a prenuptial agreement— no litigation, no fear of the stock being overvalued at a trial, and no disclosure of private family finances—would almost always be accomplished by a liquidity agreement.
- It reduces pressure by the uninvolved minority shareholders to declare dividends when the cash might be better used for expansion. Dissatisfied shareholders will

either sell their stock or, if they know they can sell their stock and are not being forced to hold an illiquid asset, will be less suspicious of how the company is being run.

- It reduces pressure from the uninvolved shareholders to have the company adopt other kinds of strategies that show immediate results.
- It reduces management's reluctance to adopt long-term strategies for fear that the noninvolved shareholders would be impatient.
- It requires that management reserve cash to fund prospective buyouts, thus preventing management from paying themselves excessive salaries or otherwise depleting the company's working capital.
- It can provide a remedy for the problems created by an estate plan that gives corporate control to uninvolved shareholders by treating the children equally. If a business owner's will divides her stock equally among her children, a liquidity agreement can protect the child running the business by giving the uninvolved siblings an opportunity to liquidate their holdings without punishing the child who runs the business. When everyone is communicating well *and* a liquidity plan is in place, equal ownership can be a virtue, by reducing the resentment caused by some family members having more long-term benefits than others.

Prenuptial Agreements—Shortcomings and Alternatives

The prospect of a marriage should present a situation of great joy. However, for the members of a business-owning family, marriage sometimes has the potential to create considerable anxiety. What if the marriage doesn't work? Will our new son or daughter-in-law want to get stock in the business? How much of the family business finances (which we have kept secret from the industry) will their divorce proceedings make public? Disclosure of our margins would give our competitors a great advantage. The common wisdom is that a prenuptial agreement can address many of these concerns.

However, these agreements often do not provide the expected benefits, and what benefits they do provide might be better achieved by other means that have far less emotional cost.

Costs versus Benefits

Lawyers and consultants who have negotiated prenuptial agreements between young people marrying for the first time will verify that they are in fact sometimes hard negotiations, and not collaborative efforts between two people who easily come to an understanding. Rather, they often involve painful discussions requiring those two young people to condition their love and commitment to marriage on an arrangement concerning money.

People who have been married before and have adult children or grandchildren to whom they have financial commitments may find this negotiation easy and helpful. But it is rarely something that people under the age of thirty wish to contemplate, let alone negotiate.

If parents are pressuring their child to negotiate a prenuptial agreement, it can put incalculable strain on the young couple's relationship. While most children want their parents' approval and encouragement about their decision to marry, healthy children come to that decision independently of their parents. Having parents insist that the children negotiate a contract that, from the children's point of view, seems to serve only the parents' agenda, can be infantilizing.

In addition, in the minds of spouses coming into family businesses, there must be the concern that although their prospective in-laws appear to be welcoming them into the family as full-fledged members, there seems to be some mistrust, and the in-laws seem more concerned with money than whether the newlyweds are beginning their marriage on a healthy footing.

The expected benefits most often used to justify prenuptial

agreements are that they will (a) prevent protracted court battles that expose the family's finances; (b) keep the family from being taken to the cleaners with high legal bills or an unfair alimony or support award; (c) ensure that the business stays in the family; and (d) avoid use of business capital to redeem stock. Yet many matrimonial lawyers would observe that in bitter divorces, these goals are rarely achieved. Prenuptial agreements are very hard to enforce. Under the law of almost every state, a prenuptial agreement is enforceable only if it is entered into without undue duress and provides full disclosure of the value of each party's assets. In fact, in some states prenuptial agreements are not enforced unless they are considered fair both when signed *and* enforced.

The "full disclosure" issue is almost always a big problem. After all, at the time that most prenuptial agreements are negotiated, no one has the incentive to make full disclosure of the value of the family business. The parents who own the business certainly do not want their in-law to know how prosperous the business is, as it may encourage gold digging or be perceived as bragging. The estate planning consultant also does not want something in writing that could be used by the IRS as evidence that the estate planning documents (which are usually premised on the lowest valuation thought to be defensible) are incorrect. Competent divorce attorneys, aware of these tendencies to undervalue the business, can wreak havoc by litigating the agreement's enforceability on the grounds of undervaluation.

The second challenge to most prenuptial agreements is that the agreement may have been entered into under duress, a *very* complicated issue. As every parent and many judges know, duress can be put on young people in all sorts of ways. Waiting to finalize the prenuptial agreement until after the wedding plans are made and the invitations sent is a classic example. Duress can be claimed regarding the many prenuptial agreements proposed shortly before the wedding, when the future spouse did not have sufficient time to review the terms.

This means that because of the many opportunities that exist to litigate prenuptial agreements, it's difficult to keep family finances a secret or save money on legal fees. If the prenuptial agreement is not generous enough for the spouse coming into the family with the business, there can almost always be issues that, if shrewdly presented to a judge, will result in there being considerable court disclosure. Thus, even if the judge does not give the incoming family member a better deal, the family will almost certainly be unable to keep its finances confidential.

Most family business owners put a high value on keeping their finances secret. They do not want to make public the salaries of the owners, the value of the business, the profit margins, or any of the hundreds of ways that many families take advantage of the tax laws. The mere threat of a trial is usually enough to negotiate a better deal than the one offered in the prenuptial agreement.

There are other ways in which prenuptial agreements can end up as costly disasters. In many states, prenuptial agreements have no effect on child support. Even if the prenuptial agreement were easily enforceable, there still can be protracted legal battles over child support that expose family finances. And it is logical to assume that merely insisting upon a prenuptial agreement can increase the likelihood of any subsequent divorce being more bitter. In many cases, the insistence upon a prenuptial agreement causes an emotional injury that may never adequately heal, especially in a marriage that does not succeed. After all, what better way to pay back the in-laws for the pain they caused when you were getting married than a court battle that promises numerous opportunities to embarrass the family?

Finally, most horror stories about the stock of the family business falling into "enemy" hands are largely apocryphal and overstated. Few people give an accurate, objective summary of what happened in a lawsuit in which they felt they were being taken advantage of or even blackmailed. On the other hand, since stock in a family business rarely pays dividends and has no real value unless the company is sold, it is doubtful that very many nonfamily members or ex-spouses genuinely want the stock for its value; rather, they seek the stock merely as a way of gaining leverage against their soon-to-be former in-laws.

Divorce lawyers will attest that judges award the stock of family business to nonfamily members or ex-spouses only under unique or the most bizarre circumstances. Certainly, few people want their cash tied up in a business that is managed by their soon-to-be-former-in-laws, who have none of the controls put upon owners of a publicly held business. People often use the threat of getting stock in the family business as a method to raise its value when the family appears to be cooking the books to create an artificially low value.

There Are Alternatives

As a practical matter, a prenuptial agreement is simply not necessary to ensure that ownership of the business stays in the family without having to buy back stock at an unfair price. A family can accomplish these goals in ways that are emotionally neutral to the young couple and more comprehensively address the core issues involving ownership of the business.

- *A buy/sell agreement.* This is an agreement signed by all the shareholders that can prohibit the transferability of stock to nonfamily members without first giving all of the family members an option to buy the stock at the price offered by the outsider or at an even bigger bargain rate. In other words, stock could not be transferred to a spouse without the remaining shareholders being first given the chance to buy it at a fair price.
- *A liquidity agreement.* The company makes a standing offer to buy the stock of any disgruntled shareholder at a price determined by a formula specified well in advance by the stockholders (see above). Since few divorcing sons- or daughters-in-law really want to own the stock of the family business, a divorce judge would likely set the stock's value according to an outside formula (applicable to all shareholders) adopted long before the divorce, in order to avoid litigation on that issue.

- *Maintaining nonmarital property status.* In many states, not all of a married couple's property is subject to division by a court upon the dissolution of their marriage. Typically, property owned by a spouse prior to the marriage, or gifted to only one spouse and not intermingled with other assets, is legally considered nonmarital property and therefore not subject to division during a divorce. Under many circumstances, the stock of the family business can be maintained as nonmarital property, and will not be subject to the divorce.

Parents who continue to reject alternatives to prenuptial agreements might merely be expressing their desire to control their children's behavior. In other words, if the parents' true motivation is to reduce legal fees, keep family finances secret, avoid the use of business capital to redeem stock from a former daughter- or son-in-law, or keep ownership of the stock among family members, these alternatives may better accomplish these goals with little, if any, emotional impact on the marriage.

Twelve Great Reasons to Have an Advisory Board

Many privately held companies are reluctant (with reason) to have a board of directors in which independent outsiders have real power. After all, it seems foolish to give independent outsiders the ability to shape the policies of a business in which they may have no stake whatsoever. On the other hand, having a board to which reports must periodically be made has a value of its own. It has become a popular best practice for privately held businesses to have an advisory board of this type. Some of these reasons may not apply to all businesses, but all of these apply to some businesses. Such a board can offer the following:

1. Provides safety if CEO dies. If a company is dominated by one person, it's hard to find a comparable senior executive with the leadership ability to take over in an

emergency. In the event of a heart attack, car accident, or other sort of sudden death, the company's entire value can diminish in a few weeks. The board can give the caretaking spouse a means to find someone to run the company in the short term until the emergency passes.

2. Diminishes the influence of an intrusive family member. Many people have strong-willed and opinionated spouses, parents, or siblings who are offended when their views about a business strategy or a child's salary or job title are not followed. Having an advisory board gives the CEO an objective means to counterbalance these people's opinions in an impersonal way.

3. Gives employees and shareholders a feeling of "adult supervision."

4. Gives objective advice on choosing successors.

5. Gives objective advice on salaries.

6. Adds expertise in areas where senior management is weak.

7. Makes the company more attractive to investors, purchasers, and lenders.

8. Provides discipline to create and follow long-range business plans, estate plans, and succession plans.

9. Keeps serious problems from being swept under rug.

10. Demonstrates that the owner/CEO has enough self-confidence to be criticized.

11. Can generate potential business opportunities.

12. Provides discipline to make hard firing decisions when necessary, abandon bad product lines when necessary, confront and correct hard times brought by bad judgment or economic turnarounds.

Six Types of Board Members to Avoid

Unfortunately, some owners of privately held businesses decide to put an advisory board into place for all the right reasons, and then compose that board of individuals who have been chosen for the wrong reasons. Board members should be chosen because of their insight, their independence, their skills and analytic abilities, and their willingness to ask hard questions.

Typically, the following types of people do not make good board members:

1. Suppliers.
2. Cronies.
3. People chosen as an award for past favors.
4. People whose perception of their own expertise makes then pout if disagreed with.
5. Potential customers.
6. Lawyers who view business decisions only in terms of potential legal risks.

Eight

Minority Shareholders' Rights

Owners of less than 51 percent of a business (a minority interest, as opposed to a majority interest) often have problems when the majority owner starts running the business in an unwise or unfair manner. Typically, this involves giving the minority owner or their children lower-paying jobs (or no job at all) or lower expense-account reimbursements. The resentment of minority owners can become even worse if they are not even employed by the business and get none of the benefits of ownership.

Imagine the frustration of a 5 percent owner of a company worth $10 million who cannot use his stake as collateral for a loan (because if the loan is defaulted, the bank could not turn his stake into cash); cannot sell his stake in the business; and gets no dividends or other advantages. In family businesses owned by second-, third-, or fourth-generation cousins, the problem can become more acute. Sometimes the minority-owner family members gets nothing other than going to one family council meeting a year where the majority family tells them how well (or poorly) the company is doing.

In some situations, getting cash flow or other benefits of ownership is the least of the problems. In a business where the minority owns a relatively large percentage, say 40 or 45 percent, the minority owners are often required by the bank to join the majority in personally guaranteeing loans. As if this situation were not bad enough, some minority owners who work for the company may also have signed noncompete agreements that prevent them from leaving the company to find a better job.

In the meantime, the minority owner's share of the business is always at risk from the majority owners' management policies, over which they have little control. The majority owners—like any owners—could threaten the company's future by implementing ill-advised business strategy, by taking out too much money, abusing expense accounts, or paying their closer family members far more than is appropriate. Certainly, this kind of behavior by the majority owner is never good for the business, sometimes it's not even good for the majority owner. Treating the minority in this way is bad management that, in the long run, will lead to other difficult problems resulting from lack of trust among the owners. But some minority owners are not merely faced with insufficient cash flow, but with personal financial ruin if the company collapses.

The Myths

Minority owners are sometimes shocked when they realize that their expectations have been shaped by some very widely held myths:

MYTH:

Owners can always sell their interest for a fair price—in other words, a 10 percent ownership interest is worth 10 percent of the value of the business.

REALITY:

Few people, if any, are interested in buying a minority interest in a nonpublicly traded company. Although it is rare, a minority owner in some circumstances might not even be able to give her interest away to anyone except a family member. In some cases, it is even possible that the ownership of a minority interest in a family business can cost that owner money. For example, if the ownership is structured as a partnership or as a subchapter S corporation, there can be a requirement to pay taxes on profits even if no cash is distributed. For reasons like this, often the *only* people interested in buying a minority interest are the majority owners!

MYTH:

The owner of a 10 percent interest is entitled to 10 percent of the business' profits and other benefits.

REALITY:

The owner of a minority interest in a business is usually entitled only to those amounts the majority owners decide to pay. Some majority owners may recognize a moral obligation to share in a way that would be considered fair. But many others do not.

MYTH:

Each owner is entitled to know all the details of what is going on in the business.

REALITY:

The owner of a minority interest is sometimes entitled to no more than a copy of the annual minutes. Sometimes, a minority owner might get financial statements summarizing the year's results. But even though minority owners have no ability to do anything based on detailed financial information, judges often frown on forcing the company to reveal these details—even to minority owners—especially when they could be used to the company's disadvantage by a competitor.

MYTH:

The owner of a minority interest in a business is entitled to a voice in its operations.

REALITY:

Although the owner of a minority interest is entitled to a voice in company operations, it is sometimes no more than a whisper. Often, minority owners may complain or criticize, or stomp their feet and hold their breath until they turn blue, but the business will continue to be run as the majority owners choose. In some limited circumstances, the minority owner may have a veto over some major transactions, but unless the business is planning one of these transactions (and unless the minority interest is large enough), this veto is of little value.

Understanding why these realities are true requires only an understanding of how corporations, partnerships, and limited liability companies are generally governed. All of these organizations have been created by a set of documents. For a corporation, they are the articles of incorporation and the bylaws. For a partnership, it is the partnership agreement. In a limited liability company, it is the operating agreement. Regardless of the names of these documents, decisions of a corporation, partnership, or limited liability company are, unless otherwise agreed in advance, made by application of a deceptively simple principle—The Majority Rules. Majority owners can unilaterally determine many things, such as the following:

- The business's employees—who they are and what they get paid. Owners of a minority stake have no right to be employed by the business, no say in who gets what job, and no ability to prevent employment of someone they do not like, even the incompetent or unmotivated child of a majority owner.
- Employees' bonuses, who gets them, and how much they get. A minority owner, even if employed, might not get the same bonus, either in total dollars or percentage of salary, as the majority owners. The minority owners have no right to get salaries or bonuses; if they are not employed by the business, they often get nothing. If they are employed and unhappy about their income, they may only have the power to quit.
- The expense reimbursements or other perks that employees receive. The majority owners may feel that a new BMW each year is appropriate for the CEO or other officers. Minority owners, even those who are employed by the business, have no right even to get the company to pay their bus fare to the annual meeting.
- Whether any dividends or other distributions are declared. The majority owners can use up all of the company's money paying themselves a salary of hundreds of thousands of dollars, providing for a new car each year, and paying for first-class travel on business trips. A 10 percent minority owner has no right to receive 10 percent, 5 percent, or any percentage of the company's earnings.

As for a minority owner getting out of this trap by selling her interest for a fair price:

- There is almost never an obligation on the part of anyone, even the majority owners, to buy the minority owner's interest. When you consider how few rights minority owners have, it should not be surprising that majority owners have little interest in buying out the minority owner. After all, majority owners, who usually are employed by the business, are often paying themselves the salary they want and are giving themselves the cars, vacations, offices, and travel that they want. Since they already have everything that the company can afford to give them, why should they invest money into buying more ownership interest when they don't need it?

- It is true that if the company is sold, the owner of 10 percent of a company is entitled to 10 percent of the proceeds. But this applies only to the proceeds left over after the majority owners have received the extra money that is often paid to key employees in exchange for their agreement to consult for or not compete with the new owners. Thus, in return for their promise to provide consultation or their promise not to compete in the future, the majority owners can get 10 percent, and sometimes up to 20 percent, of the entire package in a form that is not considered purchase price. If the majority owners take 20 percent off the top, the 10 percent minority owner will end up with only 8 percent of the proceeds.

- The reality of how the distributions are made in the event of a sale sometimes discourages the majority owners from distributing dividends to the minority owners. Rather, they choose to reinvest the cash into the business. Although this may appear to be a virtue at first glance, it is another way for the majority owners to take advantage of the minority owners. Majority owners get more leverage by having the business's excess cash reinvested, not distributed. Assume that the 60 percent majority owners know that they would get 70 percent of the proceeds from the sale of the business (because of noncompete agreements, consulting agreements, and the like). If the business distributes money pro rata before a sale, the majority owners get 60 percent of it and the minority owners get 40 percent. If the majority owners make the company reinvest the money, the majority owners will eventually get 70 percent of it upon a sale and would also get 70 percent of any increase in the value of the business that is the result of this reinvestment. Even if the reinvestment is good for the business and sometimes for the minority owners, it will be even better for the majority owners.

When the minority owners are treated unfairly, they often jump to the conclusion that this treatment is personal, especially if the majority owners are family members. But unfair treatment of minority owners occurs in many privately held businesses. In fact, this treatment has even been given a name. In the marketplace, this inability to sell the minority interest for its pro rata share of the business's value (that is, the inability of a 10 percent owner to sell her stock for 10 percent of the business's value) is referred to as the *minority discount*. It exists in virtually all companies.

The reasons why a minority discount exists is better understood if viewed in simple economic terms. A minority owner who wants to sell is, of course, a motivated seller. On the other hand, sometimes there is only one buyer at hand—the majority owner—and that buyer is very unmotivated. After all, the majority owner has little reason to buy unless the purchase can be made at a deep discount. The status quo is that the majority owners have everything they want—almost unlimited power to run the company and to spend its money. Why would they want to buy the stock of the minority owner and use up either their own money (which they could use to diversify their portfolios or buy summer homes) or the company's money (which they could otherwise spend on expanding the business and making it more profitable)? Acquiring an even larger portion of the business gives them almost nothing they don't have already.

The Best Solution—Talk Out the Problem and Resolve It Fairly

There are many ways to resolve this situation provided everyone is willing to be fair, respectful, and rational about how much trouble the minority and majority can cause each other. But "fair" is a moving target and, in family business situations, it is all too often clouded by family history and resentments. It's common in situations like this for the owners, who are angry and frustrated, to resolutely and rigidly announce a "non-negotiable" position that makes compromise difficult.

There are lots of ways to resolve this situation, but usually a solution first requires that the owners see their disagreement as being *only* about money! The minority owners who want to be bought out must recognize that they will have to agree to a minority discount. The majority owners must realize that they are going to have to invest some of their capital into purchasing the interest of the minority owners, in order to avoid the potential damage that can be done to the business by owners trapped in an illiquid investment. These conclusions are based on economics and power, not on family history, respect, love, or any other emotion.

Agreements are usually reached only after open and honest discussions about *both* valuation and the minority owners' power to cause trouble. Often, an objective, independent outside perspective can help here. For instance, the minority and the majority owners can pursue one of these different courses:

- Hire separate investment bankers or accountants to research the marketplace in order to determine the value of the business and the typical minority discount for that industry. Ideally, these professionals would then honestly and candidly talk to each other and recommend an appropriate compromise.

- Hire a professionally trained mediator to facilitate a rational and honest discussion. Good mediators never take sides, try to decide who is right, or blame someone for the impasse. Rather, they help maintain a dialogue in which everyone stays rational and on task.

- Appoint a trusted *neutral* friend or advisor empowered to make a decision that everyone agrees in advance to accept. "Neutral" requires that the person has no stake whatsoever in the outcome. For example, the company's accountants or lawyers are almost never neutral. They may not own stock, but they still have a stake in the outcome. In other words, one outcome might mean that they go on working for the company, while a different outcome could mean that they are replaced.

- Agree to binding arbitration. This means that the parties agree to have someone else decide on the price of the stock. This can be very helpful, but is often very expensive because the presentation to the arbitrator is often as long and detailed as a trial. Nevertheless, as expensive as it might be, it is usually less expensive than litigation.

When Talking Fails

If the talking does eventually fail, the majority owners and the minority owners are usually even angrier with each other than they were when the talking started. This anger, if left uncontrolled, leads to two situations that make a bad problem even worse.

The first is that the angry minority owners choose a lawyer who promises to give them the emotional satisfaction of revenge. In other words, instead of choosing a lawyer who will devise a cool-headed strategy for getting the best price, they choose a lawyer who tells them how horribly they have been wronged and promises to be a vicious street fighter to help them punish and get even with the people who so abused them. This is almost always a mistake. The eventual goal in these situations is to make the majority owners realize that they should offer more money in order to avoid the risk of a trial. It does not help the majority owners reach this realization if the minority owner's lawyer behaves in a vindictive and hostile manner. Howard T. Markey, the Chief Judge of the United States Court of Customs and Patent Appeals, in speaking to graduates of the Dickinson School of Law, noted that, "We need not one more lawyer who cannot disagree without being disagreeable . . . Peacekeeping is not surrender. On the contrary, it takes a special skill . . . to see that the best true interest of your client lies outside the courtroom . . . Indeed, peace itself requires advocacy." This is especially wise advice for lawyers involved in family business disputes.

The second unfortunate result of letting this kind of anger become the subject of negotiations is that it prevents the minority owners (and sometimes the majority owners) from understanding that the disagreement is not about family—it's about money. Ultimately, the decision to compromise and resolve the dispute has to be made by the owners themselves, not by the lawyers. Unchecked anger warps the ability to be rational and understand when the best price has been "won." The issue for minority owners should be how much money they can get without incurring inappropriate risk or expense; it should not, and should never be, how much pain or punishment they can inflict on the majority owners.

Unfortunately, sometimes these discussions become bitter arguments about what is fair, what is just, what is right, what happened years ago, or what Mom and Dad would have wanted. No agreement about price is reached, and lots of resentments and painful memories get stirred up. Sometimes these "negotiations" are so bitter that they make compromise less probable.

But no matter how nasty the discussions become, the majority owners still have no reason to buy, unless they can purchase the minority interest at a severe discount. The minority owners, on the other hand, feel angrier and angrier—both at the cash flow being provided by the business to the majority owners and by their inability to raise the price being offered by the majority owners. The minority owners' frustration is often exacerbated by the fact that the majority owners' team of lawyers, accountants, and consultants is being paid by the business, whereas the minority owners have had to pay for their consultants out of their own pockets.

In these situations, the minority owners come to realize that the only question has become, "What, if anything (other than lowering my requested purchase price), can I do to motivate the majority owners to pay more money for my ownership interest?"

The answer to this question is not always clear. But at some point a minority owner needs to think of the situation as if the majority owner owns a goose that is laying golden eggs, all of which are going into the pocket of the majority owner. If the majority owner refuses to share any of the golden eggs with the minority owner, the minority owner's best *tactic* (once asking, yelling, and begging have failed) may be to threaten to kill the goose.

Many people might say that this is irrational, destructive, childish, or vindictive. They might also say that this is "destroying your family's heritage" or "desecrating Granddad's legacy." On the other hand, someone might suggest that both the family heritage and Granddad's legacy have already been violated by the majority owners' decision to keep all the benefits for themselves.

How does one go about pursuing this option? When the question is posed in this manner, the answer starts to become clear: consult a lawyer about filing a lawsuit that threatens the existence of the business. The first question, of course, is what kind of a lawsuit can do that?

- *Statutes* Many states have statutes that provide remedies for minority owners of corporations. (Although these examples pertain to corporations, minority owners of partnerships or limited liability companies often have similar protections.) A California statute provides for involuntary dissolution of a company if those in control have allowed "persistent and pervasive fraud," or "mismanagement, abuse of authority, or persistent unfairness toward any shareholders," or if the company's "property is being misapplied or wasted by its directors or officers." An Illinois statute provides that if the corporation assets are being "misapplied or wasted," a judge can remove a director or officer, appoint a custodian to manage the business, require the purchase of the shares of the minority shareholder for their "fair value," or dissolve the company. Statutes such as these are common, but not universal. The laws of New York and Delaware, for instance, do not give minority shareholders these broad rights.

- *Fiduciary Duties* Another type of claim is one in which the minority shareholders assert that the directors, officers, managing partners, or the majority owners have breached their "fiduciary duty" to the minority owners. A fiduciary duty is lawyerspeak for describing the highest possible standard of honesty and care. Each officer and director of a corporation, and often the majority owner, owes a fiduciary duty to the business and sometimes its owners. A person's fiduciary duty prohibits all self-dealing. Examples of possible breaches of fiduciary duty would be loans of excessive amounts with inadequate collateral or at lower-than-market-rate interest; personal use of company money (for example, having the company employees perform the president's home swimming pool maintenance, purchasing art for the president's home, or payment for family vacations); pocketing personal profit from business opportunities that could have been exploited or enjoyed by the company; or competing against the company.
- *Failure to Manage* Under some circumstances, a lawsuit can be brought if the majority owners are also officers of the company and are not doing their job. A majority owner who is president of the company, but who takes

five months of vacation and spends much of the rest of the time in his office managing his personal portfolio, can be at risk of having a judge order that he be fired from his job as the result of this type of lawsuit.

- *Derivative Actions* Some claims can be brought as a "derivative action," where the minority shareholder's ability to sue is "derived" from the company. In other words, if the corporation is paying an excessive salary to its president, the corporation must sue, because it (and not the shareholder) is being harmed. The law recognizes that a company's president will not authorize the company to bring the lawsuit, and thus sometimes allows a shareholder to bring the suit.

- *Squeeze Out or Oppression* This type of lawsuit claims that the majority owners are trying to "squeeze out" or oppress the minority owners by abusive tactics designed to force the minority owners to sell their ownership interest at below its fair value. This type of lawsuit can be used in those circumstances where majority owners actually change corporate policies to make minority ownership less attractive.

- *Deadlocks* States often have statutes that give a judge the power to dissolve a corporation in the event that the shareholders are so deadlocked that they cannot elect directors, or the directors are so deadlocked that they cannot appropriately run the business. However, deadlocks do not occur as often as one might think. Usually, they require that the ownership be divided 50/50 or that one faction of the ownership simply refuses to make a decision. For example, ownership could be divided 40/40/20, with the 20 percent owner simply refusing to take part in a decision.

Any lawsuit that raises these issues or that seeks this type of relief will be expensive. Lawyers will charge large hourly rates and get large fees. The majority owners may hire very high-end lawyers who will be paid by the business itself and may charge hundreds of thousands of dollars in fees.

But the issue here is not what the lawyers will get. The issue is what the minority owners are willing to invest to raise the price being offered for their minority interest. By this point, one thing should be certain: talking has failed! If minority owners do nothing, they will get nothing. The rational question is, "Will the investment of $5,000 or $50,000 or even $500,000 in legal fees increase the price being offered by 10 percent, 20 percent, 50 percent, or more?"

Minority owners are often very bothered by the fact that the majority owners seem to be paying massive legal fees by using company funds. However, this may actually be to the advantage of the minority owners. After all, the money going to the lawyers was not going to the minority owners in the first place. On the contrary, it is money that would have been financing the company's growth or going to the majority owners to pay for fancy cars and large salaries. The fact that the business hires a big firm with high rates may be simply reducing the size of the golden eggs that only the majority owners are getting.

"But," you might say, "my goal is to have my interest bought— not to have the company dissolved. You told me I have no right to make them buy my interest. How does the dissolution of the company or disqualification of the majority owners as officers help me, a minority owner, get a higher price?"

First of all, "dissolution" does not really mean "dissolution." What it means is that the company will be sold. This is not as draconian as it may seem. After all, if the company is sold, who is the most likely buyer? The majority owners; no one else knows the business as well as they do, no one has as much information, and no one wants it as badly. Dissolution means that the majority owners would be forced to find financing or a new partner (who, presumably, negotiates financial restraints in advance). Since they are buying the company, they can hardly pay themselves for consulting or not competing. Unlike in a sale to a third party, a sale to the majority owners may give the minority owners a pro rata portion of the proceeds.

Second, if the majority owners are disqualified as officers, they lose their jobs, and this is a risk most majority owners will not take.

"But," you might say, "I have consulted with a lawyer about this, and the lawyer said I can't force anyone to buy my stock and I have very little chance of winning a case for dissolution, disqualification, squeeze out, or breach of fiduciary duty. Shouldn't I take the lawyer's advice and just wait longer?"

Maybe. Most lawyers will honestly tell you when they are not optimistic about winning. After all, the words of statutes have no single precise meaning, and lawyers' research will show that few minority owners have "won" cases like this. Their pessimism is both rational and appropriate.

To some extent, this pessimism is the result of the wrong question having been asked. The critical question that lawyers should be asked in a situation like this is not, "Can I be sure of winning?" At this point in time, a minority business owner should know, without needing a lawyer, that they cannot be sure of winning. The critical question to ask a lawyer is, "Will the majority owners be sure of winning?"

The good news about all this uncertainty is that eventually the majority owners' lawyers will tell them the same thing your lawyer told you: they, too, are not sure of winning. The lack of precise meaning is *exactly* what will create, in the minds of the majority owners, ambiguity about the business's future and anxiety about the possible consequences of your claim. And sometimes, minority owners find out that their chances of "winning" are greater than they thought. Once they show their resolve by filing a suit, the majority owners often become more reasonable. After all:

- They may want to avoid the possibilities of permanent family fractures, tarnishing the family's reputation, or the exposure of family business finances that will inevitably occur during a lawsuit.

- Many privately held companies bend rules in their income tax reporting, and most judges have little tolerance when it comes to tax cheats. This fact alone would cause a judge to lean heavily toward letting you end your forced investment in a company that cheats on its income tax.
- Judges, in general, will often try to resolve family disputes. Judges have many tools to encourage compromise, especially in family business disputes. Many judges will try to figure out what the marketplace might deem as fair and then pressure both sides to compromise near that point.
- Oftentimes, the greed of majority owners unwilling to act fairly is manifested in other ways. For example, the salaries they pay themselves or their children may be deemed abusive by industry standards when compared to profitability of the company.
- The expense account reimbursements of the majority owners may be typical of what their friends get from other privately held companies, but will seem abusive to judges or jurists who don't drive fancy cars, don't fly first class, and don't have vacations paid for by a company.
- Sometimes it can be shown that the majority owners' children are being paid without regard to the quality of the work they are doing.
- A smoking gun can sometimes be found in the private communications (emails, etc.) of the majority owners with the company's lawyers or accountants, where they explicitly seek advice on how to take advantage of the minority owners. In situations such as this, there is a chance that communications to the lawyers or accountants can be disclosed to an unhappy shareholder.

In these cases, pursuing a lawsuit is like horseshoes: getting close can be good enough. Your aim is to create enough anxiety, uncertainty, fear, or ambiguity in the minds of majority shareholders so that they pay a higher price to buy you out than they would have otherwise. They will pay you more money in order to avoid the risk (even if it's a small risk) of incurring a devastating loss at a trial. "Winning" does not necessarily mean that a verdict be entered for you in a lawsuit—it means getting a higher price for your ownership interest. An apocryphal story about two friends camping in Alaska may help explain. They were sitting around the fire discussing what they would do if a grizzly bear were to attack them. One said that he had read that if that happens, the only chance of survival is to roll up in a ball and hope that the bear simply scratches you a little before going on to other more interesting prey. The other friend just stared into the fire and, after a long wait, said, "If that happens, I'll start running." His friend responded, "That's nuts! You can't outrun a grizzly bear." The wiser one said, "I don't have to outrun the bear, I just have to outrun you."

In addition, the majority owners will find out that while the lawsuit (and appeal, if you do lose) is pending, the business will have to operate under a cloud that prevents them from doing whatever they want. Their bank will look at their behavior more suspiciously, maybe restricting the amount of money that is available to them or requiring more collateral for loans. It might refuse to renew a loan until the dispute with the minority is resolved. Transactions like acquisitions, which might be vital to the business, may have to be put on hold. The company's ability to raise new capital is diminished or suspended until the lawsuit is resolved. And, most certainly, all expenditures are potential evidence that will be reviewed by the judge.

Although it may take years, the majority owners will eventually come to grips with the situation and begin to realize that they have many reasons to pay minority owners a higher price. In some respects, they are in a no-win situation. Losing at a trial (even if they have only a 20 or 30 percent chance of losing) is a disaster, while winning simply puts them back to where they were before (minus their legal fees). They have nothing to gain and almost everything to lose. The minority owners, on the other hand, have almost nothing to lose (just their attorneys' fees) and a great deal to gain. Eventually, the majority owners realize that they are on the wrong side of the risk-benefit analysis and find that purchasing the minority interest for a higher price than previously offered is a rational way out of their dilemma.

Can These Situations Be Avoided?

Can this all be avoided before a dispute over price occurs? Of course! Early in the business's development, before the goose has started laying golden eggs, before the offending practices have begun or before there are so many owners that the negotiations are endless, the owners can enter into an agreement. Or, they can enter into agreements later in the business's development, as long as the parties are advised by lawyers, accountants, and other consultants who see that everyone accommodates each other owner's power.

The majority owners are entitled to impose a minority discount. This is not an issue of family. It's simply an issue of economics that is present in all businesses. On the other hand, the minority owners also have the ability to cause a great deal of trouble to an abusive majority and should be given an "exit strategy" if they want or need liquidity. For their part, majority owners should commit to behave in a way that earns the trust of the minority owners.

Creating a well-written and well-reasoned agreement that reflects and addresses each party's concerns is time-consuming, expensive, and requires patience from all parties concerned. It will have serious legal and tax consequences and should be accompanied with a serious commitment to get it right. Even when the owners are siblings who have the utmost trust in each other, this is not a do-it-yourself project that can be completed on a kitchen table by a form downloaded from the Internet or by using an agreement that someone else's business found helpful.

Although I haven't attempted to provide a comprehensive list of every provision or arrangement that can be made, here are some examples of issues that should be considered:

1. *Requirements for distribution of cash.* Some businesses have solved the issue of minority owner liquidity by requiring that majority owners' salaries and benefits be limited so that some cash can be distributed to the minority owners. Another common arrangement is to require that cash be paid to the minority owners in proportion to the bonuses or other compensation paid to the majority owners or employees of the business.

2. *Details for shareholders.* Sometimes all it takes is a steady supply of detailed information to alleviate minority owners' frustration. In this way, the minority owners can be reassured that the business is being run in a rational and sensible way.

3. *Limitations on consulting and noncompete arrangements if the business is sold.* As discussed, the majority owners' ability to receive large consulting or noncompete payments changes their motivations for reinvestment and selling. Limiting such payments or agreeing that they will be shared among the owners pro rata often helps generate an atmosphere of fairness.

4. *Minority buyout option.* Under the worst of circumstances, majority shareholders could reject a sale with exceedingly favorable terms because it would mean that the majority owners would lose their jobs. To avoid this, the shareholders could agree that the minority could be given the right to name a price at which the majority owners must either buy the minority interest or sell majority control to the minority owners.

5. *Opportunities to be bought out at a predetermined formula.* Owners of privately held businesses sometimes can agree that the business's value is related to the value of a publicly traded competitor. In other words, some privately held companies conclude that if the stock market values a publicly traded competitor at ten times' earnings, that should also be the value of the privately held company. Once this value is fixed and a minority discount established (both of these agreements are easier to reach if negotiated prior to stock being distributed or in advance of a dispute), the business

could be obligated by a contract to have a certain percentage of its annual earnings available to buy back stock of minority owners who would rather invest their money elsewhere.

6. *Arrangements for orderly management of the business in the event of a majority owner's death.* Succession planning is important for all businesses at all times. It is in everyone's best interest that there be an arrangement for the orderly transfer of power to a qualified successor in the event of the unanticipated death or disability of the majority owner.

7. *Require an independent board of advisors or directors that has a veto power over some of the majority's actions.* One of the many virtues of an independent board of directors or advisors is that its presence often helps the minority owners avoid oppression by the majority, and helps resolve an unfair situation if it occurs. Usually, by focusing only on the health of the business and not on any owners' short-term desire for wealth, an independent board helps all the owners reach solutions that are good for both the business and the owners.

8. *Know the minority rights before the ownership entity is created.* There are, of course, exceptions to the governance policy of The Majority Rules. Different types of entities and different states have different protections for minority owners. The differences among these, however, are so important that they should govern what type of legal entity owns the business and in what state it is created. For instance, under certain circumstances, a 10 percent partner has dramatically more rights than the owner of 10 percent of a corporation's stock. Some states give majority owners far more power than other states. That is one reason so many large companies are Delaware corporations. Sadly, the importance of the choice of entity is usually realized too late—after a dispute has arisen.

Lawsuits are never fun. They almost never result in clear-cut winners or losers, and always cause emotional strain for the participants. Nevertheless, lawsuits are sometimes the only way to solve a problem or resolve a dispute. But it should always be remembered that lawsuits are not wars. They are not about exacting revenge.

Rather, they are a dispute resolution mechanism paid for by the government (the courts) in which a third party (a judge) makes a decision in an otherwise irreconcilable dispute.

The best advice is to always remember that it's not about love, respect, or revenge. On the contrary: it's just about money.

▶ *Nine*

Estate Planning—Some Forgotten Goals

Some lawyers, accountants, and insurance salespeople who are experts in estate planning have been trained to think that estate planning starts and ends with tax savings or financial planning. They think (and are often asked by their clients to think) only about reducing taxes or making sure there will be enough wealth for a surviving spouse. Sometimes, this focus coincides with a product or service that the advisor is selling. Insurance salespeople naturally want to sell insurance and will see quickly and clearly what insurance policies are necessary so that a surviving spouse has enough cash to live on. Financial advisors will understand the consequences of surviving spouses making ill-advised investments of their inheritances.

For their part, some lawyers think only in terms of tax savings and protecting money from the imagined greed of sons-in-law or daughters-in-law. In fact, since good estate planning is expensive, clients sometimes evaluate their fees by the amount of taxes that were saved.

Unfortunately, many experts fail to offer any guidance on two significant issues: first the emotional impact that the estate plan will have on the survivors, and second, when a business is the principal asset of an estate, whether ownership of that business will be structured to promote that business's continued health. As a result, many estate plans result in the maximum saving on taxes, provide an abundance of insurance proceeds for the widow, and guarantee that skilled advice will be given as to how to invest those proceeds. Yet, these plans can inadvertently create and foster family tensions around

■ *143*

how the assets were distributed or lead to the demise or stagnation of the family business because of how its ownership was structured.

It is easy to see how the relationship between children and the surviving parent or siblings can be adversely affected by the manner in which the estate plan distributes the assets. For example, if a mother leaves the bulk of her estate to one of her two daughters, there is a good chance that jealousy and resentment might prevent them from having a healthy relationship after their mother's death. Similarly, people involved in second marriages sometimes leave their children's inheritance up to the discretion of their stepmother or stepfather. This can lead to serious resentments and tensions among the survivors.

Although the impact on the business is subtler, it is just as real. Leaving ownership of the business divided among four siblings may seem like a good idea. However, if only one of those siblings has ever been involved in the business, and if the other three have always been jealous of that sibling's special relationship with their father, it is safe to predict that this jealousy will show itself when decisions have to be made about the future of the business.

The reason for this oversight is simple—lawyers, financial advisors, insurance salespeople, and accountants, like people in all other professions, feel most comfortable focusing on things they understand and problems they have the skills to solve. After all, as I noted earlier, "When a hammer is your only tool, every problem looks like a nail."

Of course, this does not mean that you should avoid these types of experts; estate planning with the traditional tax and financial focus can save considerable amounts in taxes and provide the surviving spouse with financial security through wise investments.

What this does mean is that, like in all other dealings with your lawyers or other consultants, you must be the boss. You need to supervise your estate planners so that they will focus on your goal of avoiding the emotional problems created by a poorly thought-out estate plan, and balance this goal with the more typical financial goals.

First, Do No Harm

Young doctors are taught that one of the most important principles of practicing medicine is "First, do no harm." To avoid harm,
you and your advisors need to consider what will happen after
your death as a result of the decisions you've made while you were
alive. And, like all things that require looking into the future and
predicting how people will act, it is never easy. Still, it is well worth
the effort for your family's sake.

There is no formula or roadmap for success in this area. Rather,
it requires that you explain to your advisors not only your financial
goals, but also your personal priorities. Then, you must supervise
their work to make sure that it fulfills all of your goals and priorities, not just the ones that your advisors are most comfortable
with. Your effort can be guided by three simple insights.

Don't be afraid to talk about it

Talk to your children about your plans. Yes, it's hard to discuss
either your death or your money or both with your children, especially when you, like so many other people, are convinced you
will never die. And yes, you don't want to destroy their ambition
by telling them that they will come into what might be a large
inheritance. But only by discussing this with them before you die
can you make sure that they know your thoughts and reasoning.
The chances of their having seriously hurt feelings or tension with
their siblings or surviving parent is dramatically higher if they are
left to guess at why you did what you did and how it reflects on
your feelings about them. They may not like your decisions, or they
may not agree with your logic, but if they hear it from you, they
are most likely to accept it without blaming their other parent or
siblings.

If you are leaving the family business to one child or to all your
children, explain why. And listen to their reaction. These might
teach you something.

If you are leaving the family business to the child who has worked for it, and you are giving it to her at a bargain price because of the value she created, explain this to your other children. After all, she earned it by adding considerable value, or working for years for less money than she might have made elsewhere. But, unless the other children hear that from you, they might never understand your feelings about it, and the ensuing resentment could smolder for years.

If you are leaving your wealth spread equally among your children, explain why you did this. After all, your son who is a grammar school teacher might resent that he did not get a larger share of your estate since he needed the money so much more than your daughter who is a successful lawyer. It is better for him to hear it from you while you are alive than to stew about the issue after you have died. Similarly, if you leave more money to one child than to another because of a specific problem (such as your son having a disabled child), you should explain this decision to those of your children who got less because they had no children or were blessed with healthy children.

The fact is that no matter what you do, it is always better if your children hear the logic of your decision from you and are not left to incorrectly interpret your reasoning or feelings.

Don't be penny-wise and pound-foolish

Although normally it is best to pay taxes as late as possible, sometimes more money can be made if you pay taxes early. Paying an estate tax early, even though it may seem foolish, can be a wise investment if it increases the opportunities for the family business to succeed over the long run.

For example, married people can leave an unlimited amount to surviving spouses without taxes. Thus, a man with a family business worth $6 million might be advised to leave the stock of that business to his widow even though the man's daughter runs the business and is recognized as his successor. Certainly, this plan has merit. The mother will hold the stock while she is alive, be able to avoid taxes by gifting some to her daughter, and then pay the estate tax when she dies and the remainder of the stock passes to the daughter.

Yes, this does save money by avoiding the unnecessary early payment of taxes. The mother might live for another ten to twenty years and during that period someone will be making money on the taxes that would have been paid if the stock had gone directly to the daughter when her father died. Well, then, how could this be a bad plan?

It might not be, but the question is, will the mother be a good owner or a good boss? Even though the father may have intended his widow to merely hold the stock and not have any opinions, the rest of the world will see her as the owner. The company's bank will require her to approve any new financing for the business and possibly to personally guarantee the company's loans. Will she do that? Will she see the need or wisdom of a new loan for an expansion of the factory? Will she agree with and trust her daughter's judgment that even though spending money on expansion is a risk, not expanding is a greater risk because it could cause the company to lose sales to its largest competitor? Conversely, will the mother insist on taking working capital from the company in the form of a salary or dividends? If she becomes afflicted with dementia, will the daughter need to have a conservator appointed for her mother so that decisions can be made? Will the mother understand her daughter's desire for a larger salary? Will she be able to give the sympathy and support that even senior executives sometimes need from their boss?

If the mother fails at any of these jobs, what effect will it have on the business or on her relationship with her daughter? If the business begins to falter, will she blame her daughter? Will they fight if the mother is slow to make decisions? Will the daughter want to sell the business and look for another career because of the problems of dealing with her mother? If any of these things happen, the financial consequences (not to mention the impact on the personal relationship) will be far worse than paying the taxes that would have been imposed if the father had merely left the stock outright to his daughter.

Don't forget the principles of good management

Anyone who has ever had partners or worked with co-owners knows that these are not easy relationships. The controlling owners have interests that often differ from and are sometimes at odds with those of the minority owners. Often the majority owners work in the business and every dollar of salary or expenses that they are paid is not available to be distributed to the minority owners. Decisions about whether to sell the business also affect the employed owners differently from the "silent" owners. Using capital to expand the business, as opposed to distributing it among the owners, also can cause tension.

Thus, the manner in which a business owner distributes the stock of the company can have a profound impact on how the company is managed in the future. For example:

- Many husbands who own businesses, and whose principal income is a salary from that business, agree to an estate plan that leaves their surviving spouse with that same salary. To do this, they often leave ownership of the company to the surviving spouse so that she can make sure she gets a salary or other distributions. Unfortunately, this sometimes harms the business, because paying a salary to a person who adds little value amounts to a loss of liquidity. Also, if a child running the business is prevented from making forward-looking decisions, he may become frustrated enough to sell—or worse, quit the business. The goal of providing regular income to the surviving spouse might better be achieved by purchasing insurance to provide this income, while leaving the ownership to the child already involved in the business. One would think that most adult children would gladly pay for such insurance if they knew they would later own the business outright without having their widowed mother as a boss.

- Likewise, treating the children equally does not require that the ownership of the family business be divided equally among several children. This is especially true if equal treatment results in the children directly involved in the business becoming minority shareholders who may forever need the approval of their sisters and brothers for major decisions. Few things are more likely to cause tension and irrational decisions than the business leader not having control. Realizing that the future of the business may depend on unequal treatment does not mean that the children will be treated unfairly. In fact, this can often be a wise legacy. If there are not enough assets in the estate to leave an appropriate inheritance to each child, financial planning can help remedy that situation, either by providing liquidity through insurance or taking money from the business to be inherited by the noninvolved siblings.

- Showing respect, love, and appreciation to a second wife does not require that she become the trustee of a trust fund left for the children of a first wife. The creation of a trust, by itself, almost always evokes an emotional reaction on the part of the people that the trust was intended to benefit. The choice of trustee can have a huge impact on the nature and strength of that emotional reaction. Choosing a trustee without regard to the emotions of the beneficiaries can almost be assured of creating serious problems.

The Basics

Estate planning is the process of determining how a person's assets will be distributed upon their death and how to reduce the taxes that are imposed on this distribution. There are two basic insights that govern the tax savings that are possible through estate planning: first, the taxes imposed are about 50 percent (or more) of the value of any person's estate that exceeds $1.5 million (this threshold will increase to $2 million in 2006 and $3.5 million in 2009). Thus, in 2005, a person can, upon his or her death, distribute $1.5 million to anyone they choose, tax-free. This amount is commonly called the *unified credit*. Wealthy individuals should, if possible, transfer this amount to their children (or a trust for their children) and not to their spouse, thereby avoiding this money becoming part of their spouse's estate and thus taxed upon their spouse's death.

Second, an unlimited amount can pass to a person's spouse without taxation. This is called the *marital deduction*.

Thus, if planned appropriately, a married couple can, in 2005, transfer $3 million tax free to their children by each parent leaving his or her $1.5 million unified credit to their children.

Nevertheless, for those married couples whose wealth exceeds twice the unified credit, the estate taxes can be considerable. A married couple with assets of $5 million in 2005 faces potential estate taxes upon their death of about $1 million (50 percent of $5 million, less the combined unified credit of $3 million). A couple with assets of $10 million faces potential estate taxes in 2005 of about $3.5 million (50 percent of the difference between $10 million and $3 million).

Fortunately, even after the unified credit is fully utilized, wealthy individuals can employ two additional ways to reduce the taxes payable upon their death:

1. Freeze the value of their assets so that even if their assets grow in value, that growth will not be taxed as part of their estate. For example, imagine a couple with a $10 million net worth who spend $300,000 per year. Yet, if they are making 7 percent a year on their investments, their total estate is growing by $400,000 per year ($700,000 of earnings, less $300,000 of expenses) and their potential estate taxes could be increasing by over $200,000 per year. Sophisticated estate planning can structure the growth of these assets so that it does not get taxed as part of their estate.

2. Make the estate smaller through gifting. The government

has imposed a tax on gifts above $11,000 per person, per year. Gifts above that amount reduce the amount of unified credit available to that person upon death. Couples with children can save considerable taxes merely from annually gifting this amount. For example, a couple with three children can gift away, with no taxes whatsoever, $66,000 per year. (This is done by each parent giving away $33,000 per year, in the form of $11,000 to each of their three children.) This will result in a saving of estate taxes of about $33,000 per year (plus the added tax advantage of shielding from estate taxes the annual growth on this $66,000 per year gift).

For those who can afford to do so, gifting away part of the unified credit long before their death allows the growth of these assets to be excluded from taxation on their death. Although the law does not permit gifting away the entire unified credit, it does allow a person to gift away $1 million of their unified credit. In other words, in 2005, if a couple can afford to gift $2 million to their children (the maximum amount allowed as a reduction of the unified credit—the $11,000 per person, per year gifts are allowed in addition), the annual growth on this sum from investment will belong to the children and not be part of the parents' estate. Make note: these gifts do not need to be given directly to children. They are often given to a trust of which the children are beneficiaries.

A slightly more sophisticated manner of gift-giving is to structure gifts in a way that "leverages" the annual exemption or the unified credit into a larger amount. This is often done either by giving minority interests in a business or the economic benefit of an asset without control over it. For example, a couple that own a family business worth $10 million on its sale could give away a 1 percent interest in the stock to their son. Although he would own 1 percent of the stock, its value is far less than 1 percent of the $10 million value of the business since it is a minority interest with no control and thus subject to a minority discount. As a result, instead of it being valued at $100,000 (1 percent of $10 million), it may be valued as low as $60,000. Thus, if the stock were owned by a couple and each parent regularly engaged in gifting away stock in the company, after a few years the parents' estate could be reduced dramatically without their giving up the ability to take money out of the company in salary or diminishing their discretion to run the company as they wish. If this couple had 3 children, after 10 years they will have gifted away about 10 percent of the stock of the company, which could result in an estate tax savings of about $500,000 or more. In this way, they will have both leveraged their deduction and taken any growth on that asset out of their estate.

The Language

In doing estate planning, many people have problems understanding what is being proposed because their advisors often refer to the various techniques by using words or phrases that have very complicated and detailed meanings. In order to be involved, you must understand this jargon as if it were a new language.

Here are the terms that describe the basic building blocks of estate planning:

Will: A legal document that contains instructions about how one's estate is distributed. A will invariably requires witnesses at its signing. Wills can create trusts and generally also designate a person's choice for the guardian of their children who are still minors. When people die with a will, they are referred to as having died *testate*. If they die without a will, they are referred to as having died *intestate*.

Executor: The person appointed in a will to collect assets and see that the instructions of the will are followed. If a will states that assets are to be divided equally among a deceased's children, the executor's job is to find the deceased person's assets, determine their value, see that the taxes are paid, and then divide these assets among the children.

Estate: The whole of a person's property and debts left after death. A person's *probate estate* can be different than his or her *taxable estate*.

Bequest: A fancy word for a gift given in a will. For example, if I leave $10,000 to United Way, this is a bequest.

Rules of intestate succession: Rules that govern how a person's assets will be distributed if that person dies without a will. Each state has rules of intestate succession. When a person dies intestate, the court will appoint a person to do the same job done by an executor, called the "administrator."

Probate: The judicial process that appoints a judge to make sure that a person's probate estate is distributed properly. If a person dies with a will, the probate judge ensures that the instructions in the will are followed and that no one steals from the estate. If a person dies without a will, the probate process sees that the deceased's assets are distributed in conformance with the rules of intestate succession.

Probate estate: The part of a person's estate that is subject to the supervision of the probate court. This normally includes all property held in the name of the deceased. It would exclude property held in joint tenancy, the proceeds of insurance policies that are payable to a beneficiary, retirement funds (for example, 401K, profit sharing, IRAs, pensions, etc.) that are payable to a specified beneficiary or property in a trust. The probate process can be time-consuming and expensive (although not as time-consuming or expensive as many people fear), and various methods have been developed to avoid the involvement of a probate judge. *Joint tenancy* and *living trusts* are the principal examples.

Taxable estate: This can be thought of as simply all the money and property owned (or controlled) by people when they die. The rules that determine the size of a person's taxable estate are very complicated. The size of someone's taxable estates in the United States is governed by the U.S. Internal Revenue Code and has no direct relationship to the size of their probate estates; a person can have an estate plan that avoids there being any probate estate, yet still pay exactly the same amount of estate taxes as if their estate had been supervised by the probate court.

Trust: An agreement in which some property (the *trust estate* or *trust corpus*) is conveyed to a person or trust company (the *trustee*) who is to hold this property for the benefit of someone else. Trusts are normally created by a written document signed by the person or people creating the trust. A person creating a trust can name themselves as the trustee or appoint another individual or a company; there can also be more than one trustee. There are many types of trusts—some can last for a specific period of time (such as ten years) or until an event occurs (such as one's grandchildren reaching age forty-five).

Beneficiary: The person or persons whom the trust is to benefit. This can be a specific person ("my mother") or a group ("all my descendants" or "those of my children who are living twenty-five years after my death"). If the group is expanding, the yet-unknown beneficiaries are called the *contingent beneficiaries* (i.e., if someone creates a trust to benefit "all my descendants," that term would refer to her unborn children and grandchildren).

Trusts

Trusts are set up for many reasons, tax savings being the most obvious. Sometimes, a trust is the most useful and efficient way to see that someone has the ability and discretion to react to unforeseen events during the distribution of money. For instance, a sum of money can be left in trust for the education of a person's five children, with their uncle as the trustee who can have discretion to decide how much is spent on each.

Another common reason to set up a trust comes from doubts that a person can properly manage the money from an estate or a gift. For example, even moderately wealthy people worry that if their children inherit a large amount of money, it will either be squandered or it will destroy the children's ambition and initiative. It is certainly appropriate to worry about whether a twenty-one-year-old will wisely manage a $1 million inheritance if there are no restrictions on what can be done with the money. (However, it may be very inappropriate to do the same for a forty-year-old.)

In planning your estate, you should be aware that beneficiaries of a trust often have a negative emotional reaction if they think the trust was set up because of a lack of trust. This reaction is sometimes the result of the beneficiary misunderstanding the actual emotions of the person who created the trust. In any event, it can be of great future importance for the beneficiaries to understand the purpose of a trust and why it was chosen as a vehicle to accomplish this goal.

Here is a glossary of the various kinds of trusts and their uses:

Revocable trust: A trust that the creator (the *trustor*) can cancel at any time. Assets put in a revocable trust do not escape taxation because they are not considered to be gifts. To avoid a gift being counted as part of a person's taxable estate, that person must give up the ability to take back that gift. In other words, someone has not really given a gift of an asset if they continue to maintain the same control over that asset that they would have if they still owned it. Money given to a revocable trust is not considered a real gift since it can be taken back by revoking the trust. Nevertheless, the money in a revocable trust probably would not be part of a person's probate estate.

Irrevocable trust: A trust that cannot be revoked or changed. If properly drafted, the property in this trust will *not* be considered part of the probate estate or the taxable estate, and thus it *can* reduce estate taxes. However, many people are frustrated when they find out that irrevocable really is just that—irrevocable.

Living trust: A revocable trust that serves the same purpose as a will (by designating where the trustor's money will go after death) but avoids probate. Many trusts are set up to be revocable during the trustor's lifetime, but irrevocable upon death. The revocable trust is commonly used as a substitute for a will in order to avoid probate; however, it does not reduce estate taxes. For a living trust to be effective, the assets that are owned by the trustor must be held in the name of the trustee of the living trust.

Spendthrift trust: A trust agreement that contains provisions that prevent the money from being taken by the beneficiary's creditors.

Testamentary trust: Any trust set up by a will.

Marital trust or a general power of appointment (GPA) trust: A trust, usually set up in a will or under a revocable trust arrangement, that holds assets for the trustor's spouse that qualify for the marital deduction. Generally, these assets have not been taxed, but will be taxed upon the spouse's death. There are several classic reasons for this kind of trust. At one extreme, a husband sets it up because he does not trust his wife to make investment decisions wisely, or he wants to keep his money from being available to her next husband if she should remarry. Another reason is that in a second marriage, trustors might want the earnings on their assets to be paid to their surviving spouse upon their death, then paid to the children of the first marriage. In a typical estate plan, the marital trust holds the money (exceeding the unified credit) left to the surviving spouse. In order to qualify for the marital deduction, a trust such as this must give the surviving spouse a *general power of appointment*, which means that the surviving spouse must have the ability to appoint someone in her will who will receive these assets. Failure to provide this power of appointment might disqualify these assets from escaping tax under the marital deduction.

Qualified terminable interest ("Q-Tip") trust: A marital trust that does not have a general power of appointment, which allows trustors to give their surviving spouses a stream of income or use of an asset without the surviving spouses having a general power of appointment over the assets.

Exemption trust: A trust (also referred to as a *credit shelter trust, bypass trust,* or *family trust*) into which is placed an amount equal to the unified credit. The income from this trust can be distributed to the surviving spouse or other beneficiaries, usually children. The money in this trust can be held until the beneficiaries reach a certain age or until the surviving spouse has died. This money is exempt from estate tax since it represents the amount of the unified exemption, but if it earns money, the earnings will be subject to income taxes.

Pour-over will: A will that provides that any assets that were not put in the name of a trust will be distributed pursuant to the instructions in the will to the trustee of a designated trust (such as a trust created pursuant to a living trust). In other words, the will provides that any assets that are subject to it will "pour over" into the living trust. Even if you set up a revocable trust, you would still be well advised to have a pour-over will.

Power of attorney for healthcare/property: Power of attorney is a fancy name for a document in which an *agent* (the holder of the power of attorney) is appointed to exercise certain decisions for a *principal* (the person who signed the power of attorney). The healthcare power of attorney authorizes an agent to act for the purpose of making healthcare decisions that the principal cannot make for himself or herself. In other words, if someone is in a coma or cannot communicate effectively, the agent appointed through the healthcare power of attorney can authorize the giving or the withholding of care. The power of attorney for property authorizes the agent to act for the principal for the purposes stated in the power of attorney. These documents are often different in each state and can be very useful in the event of incapacity.

Living will: A declaration of a person's intent to have or not have his or her life artificially prolonged.

The Sophisticated Course

Many types of trusts have been created that can accomplish tax-saving goals in different and sometimes very complicated ways:

Generation-skipping trust (GST): A trust that takes advantage of tax laws that allow $1.5 million per beneficiary to skip a generation of taxation. For example, a single father who leaves $10 million to his daughter will pay a substantial estate tax (about $4.25 million). When that daughter dies, she will probably leave the assets she inherited to her children. If we assume that these assets have not grown, *another* substantial estate tax might be due. After two generations, the estate tax can total more than 70 percent. Wealthy individuals try to avoid this double taxation by leaving some money directly to the second or third generation. For example, that same single father with a net worth of $10 million could leave $3 million directly to his two grandchildren on the assumption that the $3.75 million (the approximate amount left after taxes) left to his daughter is enough. If the $3 million left directly to the grandchildren had been in their mother's estate, it would have been taxed by more than 50 percent upon her death. Trusts have been developed to manage and invest this permitted generation-skipping amount for the grandchildren, great-grandchildren, and beyond, while the income from the trust can be paid to the beneficiaries (i.e., the children and grandchildren).

Dynasty trust: A GST that is set up to go on virtually forever and thus indefinitely avoid estate taxes on the $1.5 million per person that is meant to skip generations of taxation. There is no estate or gift tax on this amount as long as the grandchildren, great-grandchildren, etc. do not take ownership of the trust assets.

Insurance trust: A trust structured to allow insurance proceeds to be paid to a beneficiary without estate taxation. This is permissible if the insurance policy is owned by the trust, as opposed to the insured. An insurance trust is created to own the insurance policy, and the beneficiaries can thus keep all of the proceeds undiminished by estate taxes. These are complicated trusts, but, if properly written and administered, they are very effective in reducing taxes.

Incentive trust: A trust set up to provide a monetary incentive for the beneficiary to behave in a certain way. For example, a trust can be established that provides beneficiaries with a lump-sum payment (say, $500,000) if they get a degree from one of a selected number of universities. Similarly, this type of trust could provide for a payment if the beneficiary got an advanced degree of a certain type (in, say, medicine). They can incentivize virtually any desired behavior.

W-2 trust: Basically, an incentive trust that gives the beneficiary a matching payment, or some multiple or fraction of the payment, based on the beneficiary's earned W-2 income. An example is a trust that pays the beneficiary two dollars for each dollar of W-2 income earned.

Voting trust: A trust that holds stock of a company that is owned by various people. The trustee can vote all of the stock. A person who controls a family business can give stock to his children (thus transferring the stock out of that person's estate), and persuade the children to put the stock in a voting trust. That way, the grantor can give the right to vote the stock to an independent trustee (thus resulting in the children having a diminished voice in the management of the business), while both the grantor and her children gain the advantage of both owning the stock and earning its growth in value, as it has been gifted out of the estate with control of the company still consolidated.

Grantor-retained income trust (GRIT): An irrevocable trust in which the grantor retains the right to all of the trust income for the *income term,* a period that ends on whichever occurs first: expiration of a fixed term or the grantor's death. If the grantor survives the income term, the trust principal (including its appreciation) passes to the grantor's beneficiaries and it will be excluded from the grantor's estate for federal estate-tax purposes. A GRIT gives the grantor the opportunity to give a leveraged gift. For tax purposes, the amount of the current gift is reduced and the growth of that amount is excluded from the grantor's estate. Also, the grantor, during the income term, has use and control of the assets.

Qualified personal residence trust (Q-PERT): A type of GRIT that allows parents to stay in their houses while the growth of the house's value is excluded from estate tax. Also, the amount of the transfer that is subject to gift tax is reduced by the value of the grantor's retained right to live in the residence for the income term. Therefore, only the present value of the children's right to receive the residence at the end of the Q-PERT term is valued as the gift.

Grantor-retained annuity trust (GRAT): An irrevocable trust designed to transfer wealth to children (or to trusts for their benefit) with little or no gift tax. Wealth transfer occurs when the assets placed in a GRAT grow at a rate faster than the IRS interest rate (or, simply, the *IRS rate*) applicable for the month in which the GRAT was created. The grantor receives annuity payments for a term of years plus interest at the IRS rate. At the end of the GRAT, trust property not returned to the grantor through annuity payments pass to the grantor's children. The size of this benefit depends on how much the actual growth rate on the GRAT assets exceeds the IRS rate. As a result, a GRAT is best suited for assets that are expected to grow at a rate well in excess of the IRS rate.

Charitable remainder trust (CRT): An irrevocable trust under which one or more individuals receive a stated amount for up to twenty years. At their death or the end of the term, the remaining trust property is distributed to charity. The CRT is used primarily to provide income security to the grantor, while, at the same time, obtaining an income tax charitable deduction. The trust may be created either during life or at death. If created during life, the grantor may be the beneficiary of the income. There are two types of charitable remainder trusts. These differ in the manner in which the stated annual amount gets paid to the noncharitable beneficiary. In a charitable remainder annuity trust (CRAT), the stated amount must be a sum certain that is not less than 5 percent of the initial fair market value of the trust. Trust distributions from a CRAT do not vary from year to year. In a charitable remainder unitrust (CRUT), the stated amount must be a fixed distribution that is not less than 5 percent of the value of the trust assets, determined annually. Distributions from a CRUT will vary each year. A CRUT may be more difficult to administer, since the trust property must be revalued every year to calculate the distributable amount.

Charitable Lead Trust (CLT): A charitable lead trust (CLT) is the flip side of a CRT. In this case, the charitable beneficiaries receive a stated amount each year for a specified term of years or for the life or lives of an individual or individuals, and at the end of the period the remaining corpus is distributed to or in trust for the grantor's descendants or other noncharitable beneficiaries. A CLT enables a person to satisfy current charitable intentions and, at the same time, transfer significant amounts of property to his beneficiaries at a reduced transfer tax cost. In times of inflation and high interest rates, CLTs are particularly effective in gaining tremendous tax savings.

► *Appendix:*

The Lawyer's Language:
A Common English Guide to
Basic Legal Terms and Concepts

Managing your lawyer so that you can make sound business decisions requires that you be able to communicate clearly with your lawyer. This means that you need to know the unique language that lawyers use when speaking about business transactions or lawsuits.

Ownership and Governance Terms

There are many forms of business ownership: partnerships, corporations, limited liability companies, limited partnerships, limited liability partnerships, and sole proprietorships. These forms differ in a number of ways:

- Whether the owner's personal assets can be taken to pay debts of the business.
- How the profits or losses are taxed.
- How profits or losses are distributed.
- Who makes decisions.
- Who has the power to dissent.
- How the proceeds of a sale of the business will be distributed.

Sole proprietorship: Merely a single person running a business. There is no business entity formed by the government and no protection granted from creditors. The sole proprietor has total personal liability for all of the business debts; income is taxed at personal tax rates.

General partnership: A partnership can be formed by two or more people. No formal written partnership agreement is required, although one is still very desirable. Two or more people who act together with a common business purpose often find themselves the subject of a court-imposed partnership which may contain provisions assumed by a judge which they never would have intended had they gone through the exercise of trying to put it in writing. Each owes a "fiduciary" duty to the other and to the business. Each is liable in total for all of the partnership's debts. In other words, Partner A can create a debt for the partnership that would have to be paid in full by Partner A *or* Partner B, even if made without Partner B's knowledge. There is no tax on the partnership. Rather, all of its income and losses "pass through" to the tax returns of the individual owners.

Limited partnership: A partnership formed according to certain technical requirements where some of the partners (the *general partners*) run the partnership and are "generally" liable for its debts. The *limited partners* have no liability for any of the partnership debts (they are only liable for the amount they agreed to pay for their limited partnership interest). However, in order to preserve this limited liability, they can have no say in the management of the venture except for preserving a veto power over certain transactions. This type of partnership works well in certain businesses, most notably real estate investment, where the investors wish to have no liability beyond their investment, the parties wish the business to be taxed as a partnership, and the investors are to have no role in making the day-to-day decisions.

Corporation: A legal entity created by a state that is managed by officers who report to a board of directors elected by the owners. The law creates a corporate democracy that allocates power within the corporate entity. In other words, the shareholders elect the directors, who then elect the officers. In the absence of an agreement by the shareholders or the directors that can be found in the by-laws or in a separate contract, the power to run the company and spend its money is allocated by state statutes between the officers, the directors, and the shareholders. Corporations have the choice of either being taxed as separate entities with separate tax rates or paying no taxes at all, with the profit and loss of the company being allocated directly to the shareholders as they would be in a partnership. Officers have very complex fiduciary duties to the corporation, as do the directors to the corporation and the shareholders to each other.

Subchapter S corporation: A corporation that elects to be taxed as if it were a partnership. In other words, a subchapter S corporation is one that has elected to have its profits and losses allocated directly to the shareholders. This election is not available to all corporations and there are restrictions on who can own stock of a subchapter S corporation.

Board of directors: Corporations (but not limited liability companies) have a board of directors elected by their shareholders. The board of directors then elects the officers. Thus, the corporation's employees report to the officers, the officers report to the board of directors, and the board of directors reports to the shareholders. Members of the board of directors have a fiduciary duty and a great deal of potential liability to the shareholders and, under some circumstances, to the company's creditors. Neither a director nor a shareholder has a right to be an employee of the company. The board of directors is sometimes called the "legal board."

Board of advisors: A group of volunteers chosen by a company or its board of directors or shareholders to advise the company's leadership. These people typically have no legal rights or responsibilities and can be retained or fired at will. They are often paid a fee for their time.

Shareholders: The people who own the stock of a corporation.

Limited liability company (LLC): A company that affords the owners (the members) the same limited liability as a corporation or limited partnership. An LLC is not taxed and its profits and losses are passed through to the members. The democracy of an LLC is set out in the operating agreement, which has great flexibility to limit the rights of the members. An LLC is typically run by managers who are appointed or elected by the members. A manager of a limited liability company can be either a member or someone who has no ownership interest in the limited liability company.

Members: The people who own a limited liability company.

Managers: An LLC does not have directors; it has managers. There can be one manager or several. Typically, the managers have power similar to that of the directors of a corporation.

Stakeholders: Those people or companies who have a stake in the success of a business. These would include the owners (shareholders for a corporation, partners for a partnership, members for an LLC), creditors, suppliers, and employees of a business.

Fiduciary duty: Imposed by law on people who are in a position of trust. Generally, it is owed to the people who have trusted them. Thus, a trustee owes a fiduciary duty to the beneficiaries of the trust, directors to the corporation and its shareholders, officers to the corporation, and majority shareholders may owe a fiduciary duty to each other or to the company which requires full disclosure of any relevant information, thoroughly honest behavior, no self-dealing, and the return of any profit made at the expense of the people to whom the duty is owed.

Finance Terms

Liquidity: The availability of cash or other assets such as stock that can be quickly converted into cash.

Net worth or book value: The difference between a company's assets and its liabilities, as shown on the company's books and records. This number has no relationship to the market value of the company. For instance, if the company buys real estate, the value of this real estate as shown on the books will usually be the cost, less the depreciation. However, the market value of that real estate could be dramatically more or less than this amount.

Balance sheet: A statement of the business's assets and liabilities on a specific date. It is a snapshot of the business that is only true on that date.

Profit and loss statement: Sometimes called an income statement or a P&L; a statement of the business's profits or losses over a specific period of time. A profit and loss statement generally shows revenue and expenses in considerable detail. If the company keeps its records on a "cash basis," only the cash receipts and cash expenditures will be shown. If the company keeps its books on an "accrual basis," the income would show invoices that have been sent but not paid and the liabilities would include bills that are due but have not been paid.

Generally accepted accounting principles (GAAP): The very detailed rules published by the accounting profession that dictate how financial information is presented in financial statements. For example, if a building is purchased for $1 million, GAAP will dictate whether it is shown on the balance sheet at its cost or at some estimate of its market value. Similarly, GAAP provide rules as to how much depreciation can be taken and how a company's inventory or work-in-process should be valued when reported on a balance sheet or when used to determine profits and losses.

Earnings before interest, taxes, depreciation, and amortization (EBITDA): Generally accepted as a more accurate reflection of a company's earnings than a profit and loss statement prepared in accordance with GAAP.

Going public: The process by which shares of stock of a corporation are registered with the Securities and Exchange Commission so that they can be sold to the general public. This is a complicated and time-consuming process that involves making full disclosure in writing of every aspect of the company's history.

Initial public offering (IPO): The event in which the company's stock first becomes available for sale to the public.

Leveraged buyout (LBO): A means by which someone can purchase a company by using the company's assets as collateral for a loan. In other words, if you wanted to buy a company for $3 million and that company owned real estate on which it could get a $2 million mortgage, a leveraged buyout would entail the company getting a $2 million mortgage on its real estate and using that money, together with the investor's $1 million, to pay $3 million to the seller.

The advantage to the investor in an LBO is that less cash is needed. The disadvantage is that the business is "highly leveraged," which means that it has a lot of debt, and one bad year or partially bad year could put the company out of business by, for example, reducing its liquidity and thus preventing it from buying raw materials that are necessary to produce new product.

Lending Terms

Promissory Note: A written promise to repay money.

Installment note: A note that is paid in installments (usually equal) of both principal and interest.

Interest-only note: A note in which only the interest is paid first, with all of the principal being due at some date in the future.

Purchase money note: A note given by a buyer to a seller to evidence an unpaid portion of the purchase price.

Balloon note: Either an installment or interest-only note, in which the last payment (the "balloon") is significantly larger than the other earlier payments.

Secured note: A note secured by a security interest (see below) or mortgage in property (either real estate or personal property).

Mortgage note: A note secured by a mortgage on real estate. A mortgage note is a type of secured note.

Floating interest rate: An interest rate that changes (or "floats") based upon certain marketplace considerations. The London Inter Bank Offering Rate (LIBOR) and the prime rate are both floating rates.

Collateral: Property that can be taken by a lender and sold if the debt to that lender is not paid.

Mortgage: A written agreement that gives a lender the right to take real estate to sell to repay a debt. The holder of a first mortgage is repaid paid first out of the proceeds of that sale. The holder of a second mortgage gets repaid out of what is left over after the first mortgage is fully paid.

Purchase money mortgage: A mortgage given to the seller by a buyer (together with a purchase money note) as collateral for an unpaid portion of a purchase price.

Security interest: The right of a lender to take property and sell it to repay a debt. A security interest is a "mortgage" on property other than real estate, such as inventory, raw materials or accounts receivable.

Security agreement: An agreement in which a borrower gives a lender a security interest in property *other than real estate* as collateral for a debt.

Purchase money security interest: A security interest given by a buyer to a seller to secure a purchase money note.

Personal liability: Typically, debts incurred by a corporation or LLC (not a sole proprietorship or a partnership) are not the personal obligation of the owners. However, these debts can become a personal obligation of the owners through their signing a personal guarantee. On these occasions, the owners are said to have personal liability.

Recourse debt: The debt of a business, such as a corporation or LLC, where the lender or creditor has recourse to the personal assets of an individual, usually an owner. Thus, the owner has personal liability for recourse debts.

Nonrecourse debt: The debt of a business where the lender or creditor has no recourse to the personal assets of any individual. In other words, no owner has personal liability for a nonrecourse debt.

Family Business Contract Terms

Prenuptial agreement: An agreement entered into by a couple about to be married in which they agree how their assets will be divided if they divorce. These agreements are not enforceable with regard to child support. Also, they are not enforceable unless both sides make full disclosure of the value of their assets and neither party signed it as the result of coercion.

Restrictive shareholders' agreement: Any agreement in which the rights of the shareholders are restricted. Some typical restrictions in family business settings:

- Transfers of stock can be made only to family members.
- Stock must be voted in a certain way with regard to electing directors.
- Stock may not be transferred to nonfamily members without first giving family members the right to purchase the stock at the same price as the outsider.

Buy-sell agreement: These agreements typically allow one shareholder to buy out another shareholder in the event of a dispute or in the event of the death of a shareholder. The agreement needs to provide for a price. Some typical provisions:

- The price is set and adjusted each year.
- The price is set by a third-party appraiser.
- The price set by one party is one that the other party can either take or leave; this mechanism is sometimes called a "shotgun."

Liquidity agreement: An agreement whereby the company commits to buy back from dissatisfied shareholders a certain number of shares each year at a preset price. This type of agreement allows dissatisfied shareholders to sell their stock at a pre-agreed price or a price determined by a pre-agreed formula, as opposed to arguing about dividend policy, officer salaries, etc. It generally encourages the management team to try to keep minority shareholders happy so as to reduce the demand to redeem stock.

Noncompete agreement: An agreement whereby employees or owners agree that for a certain period, they will not compete with the company. For example, a family business that manufactures and sells silverware might require as a prerequisite to employment that each key employee (including family members) sign a noncompete agreement prohibiting that person, even if he is fired or quits, from starting or working for a business that makes or sells tabletop products. These agreements are generally difficult to enforce and usually must be limited to a reasonable time and geographic area.

Phantom stock: An agreement between a company and an individual, or between a shareholder and an individual, that if the company is sold, the individual will receive the same amount as if she had been a shareholder. In other words, the individual can, without being a shareholder, receive the same financial benefits as a shareholder by virtue of a phantom stock agreement.

Voting trust: A trust agreement entered into by a group of shareholders where a trustee (the "voting trustee," who is typically one of the shareholders) is given the right to vote the others' shares. Thus, a person whose stock has been conveyed to a voting trust could have all the financial rights of a shareholder without any of the power since that person has given up the right to vote the stock.

Family limited liability company: An LLC where the members are family. Usually, the managers of a family LLC are the parents. Family LLCs are often created in order to obtain discounts in value so that gifts can be made for estate planning purposes or so that stock can be widely distributed among family members while leaving voting control in the hands of the company's leader.

Family limited partnership: A limited partnership in which the general and limited partners are members of a family. The general partners, the people who control the partnership's actions, are usually the parents. These are created for the same estate planning purposes as are family limited liability companies.

Litigation and Dispute Resolution Terms

Mediation: Mediation involves both parties to a dispute volunteering to allow a neutral third party to mediate a resolution. The key word is "voluntary." The mediator is neutral and has no power. Generally, people from each side who have the power to make decisions meet in a suite of offices with a mediator who either facilitates a discussion while everyone is present or carries messages, offers, and counteroffers back and forth until a resolution is voluntarily reached. Parties can leave and stop the mediation process whenever they wish. There can be no appeal to a court because no judge or jury is involved—participants make voluntary decisions. Lawyers are usually present when business disputes are mediated. Divorce mediations have also become popular and are often done without lawyers.

Arbitration: In arbitration, the parties to the dispute meet with one or more people called arbitrators, who act like judges. Juries are not used. The parties present evidence and make arguments, and the arbitrators make a decision that binds both parties. Unless there is a statute or contract that requires the resolution of disputes through arbitration, arbitration cannot be required. However, once arbitration has been agreed to, one party cannot unilaterally withdraw. Arbitrators are often lawyers or retired judges. Lawyers are almost always present during an arbitration to help present the evidence and make the arguments. There are few rules to arbitration: often evidence might be presented that would not be admitted in a courtroom; surprise is common, since there is often only a limited opportunity to find out what evidence the other side will present; there is rarely an opportunity to appeal the arbitrators' decision unless you can show that the arbitrators were biased. A decision can rarely be successfully overturned simply because it was "wrong," farfetched, contrary to established law, or unsupported by any evidence. Arbitration proceedings are normally quicker than a trial, so that the opportunity to gain advantage by delay is minimal.

Settlement: Settlement is the voluntary resolution of a dispute. Both arbitration and litigation end up with a third party deciding how the dispute should be resolved. However, in the vast majority of all disputes, including those submitted to arbitration, the parties settle, or compromise, the dispute prior to a final decision. Any mediated agreement is, by definition, a settlement because it was voluntary.

Litigation: Litigation is the process by which professional judges—either elected or appointed by the government—resolve disputes with a win-lose decision, sometimes with the help of juries. There are lots of rules and almost all of them are written down. Anyone can start a lawsuit. It is the only way to resolve a dispute if parties are unable to reach a compromise and unwilling to mediate or arbitrate the dispute. Litigated decisions can almost always be appealed.

Plaintiff: The party that initiates a lawsuit by lodging a claim.

Defendant: The party (or parties) against whom a claim is brought.

Counter-plaintiff: A defendant who files a separate claim against a plaintiff or another defendant. In other words, a defendant can be a counter-plaintiff at the same time.

Counter-defendant: A plaintiff or a defendant against whom another defendant files a separate claim.

Third-party plaintiff: A defendant who files a claim against someone other than the plaintiff.

Third-party defendant: A party who is neither the plaintiff nor the defendant against whom the defendant/third-party plaintiff files a claim.

Intervener: Sometimes a court will allow a party who is not sued to get involved in a lawsuit because the decision may affect that person's economic interests. Allowing a party to intervene in a trial is unusual. Intervention is more often done before an appellate court. A common practice before the U.S. Supreme Court, which is similar to intervention, is to allow parties to file briefs concerning decisions, which do not affect them directly, but which will affect larger questions of national economic or social policy. Briefs such as these are referred to as *amicus curae* (which is Latin for "friend of the court"). For example, in a lawsuit involving the standard of care imposed on the manufacturer of football helmets, a national trade group of manufacturers could be expected to file a brief of this sort.

Cross-claimant: Sometimes the plaintiff might choose to sue several defendants at the same time, and these defendants can be expected to have cross-claims against each other. For instance, a homeowner could find that after a new wing was built on her house, it was impossible to heat or cool that room properly. The homeowner might then sue both the air-conditioning contractor and the architect, essentially saying that the architect either specified the wrong equipment or the contractor installed the equipment improperly. Under these circumstances, both the contractor and the architect would be defendants. The contractor would become a cross-claimant if it filed against the architect, essentially saying, "If I am liable, then you should be liable to me because I did my job correctly and it was your plans that were at fault." In these circumstances, the contractor would be the defendant/cross-plaintiff and the architect would be the defendant/cross-defendant.

Complaint: The document filed with the court by the plaintiff to allege (or describe) the acts of the defendant that necessitated the claim. The complaint starts a lawsuit and determines the scope of the dispute.

Summons: The document delivered to (or "served on") a defendant, informing that party that a complaint was filed and "summoning" it to respond. A copy of the complaint is served together with the summons. The actual summons and complaint must be "served" directly on the defendant, usually by an employee of the local sheriff.

Cause of action: A legal theory that entitles the plaintiff to relief—for example, to be paid money—if certain facts are proven. For instance, the most common cause of action in business disputes is breach of contract. Simply put, a cause of action for breach of contract requires that a plaintiff prove that there was a contract with the defendant, that the defendant did not fulfill its obligations under the contract, and that the plaintiff was damaged as a result. In a business setting, another common cause of action would be a breach of fiduciary duty. An example: a member of one company's board of directors, upon hearing an idea for a new product at her daughter's swimming meet, does not tell that company, but secretly starts a separate company to sell that product. Those acts would constitute a breach of her fiduciary duty as a director of that company.

Service: The act of delivering a court paper to someone. All papers filed with the court or given to a judge must also be served on all other parties to the lawsuit. In more simple terms, it is basic to our system that no one should be able to show things to the judge in secret.

Appearance: The act of a lawyer filing an appropriate form with the court for his client. Once a lawyer "appears" for a client, all future papers are then served on the lawyer. In order for individuals to appear on others' behalf in a court, they must be licensed as lawyers.

Amended complaint: Complaints are amended to add or delete defendants or causes of action, or to add allegations to causes of action that were improperly or incompletely described initially.

Answer: The defendant's response to a complaint, counterclaim, cross-claim, or third-party complaint, intended to narrow the dispute by having the defendant either admit or deny the factual allegations made in any of those documents, or state that it does not have sufficient knowledge to either admit or deny. An answer can also assert affirmative defenses.

Affirmative defense: A set of facts or "affirmative matter" that, if proven, relieves the defendant of liability. It is not a denial that certain things happened, but rather more a statement that even if all the things the plaintiff claims to have happened *did* happen, the defendant still does not owe the plaintiff any money. In other words, if the plaintiff says, "I was walking across the street and you hit me while you were riding your bicycle," it would *not* be an affirmative defense to say, "I was not riding my bicycle at that place at that time, so I could not have hit you." An affirmative defense would be to respond by saying, "It's true that you were walking across the street, and it's also true that I hit you with my bicycle, but you walked out quickly from between two cars and you didn't look where you were walking, so I couldn't avoid you, and thus you shouldn't recover damages because of your own carelessness." Or, "The law requires you to bring this claim within two years, and it's now three years, so you are barred from bringing this claim."

Motion: A request for a judge to act. Judges almost never do things without one party first asking them to act. Most motions need to be in writing. Sometimes the judge will want briefs (written explanations or arguments) prior to deciding a motion.

Continuance: An order by the judge that extends a due date set by the court rules. Court rules usually have deadlines for when papers must be filed or actions taken. The ability to get continuances is what often makes lawyers' workloads manageable. Virtually everything can be continued with the judge's permission.

Courts of law: In general, courts of law make decisions that usually result in an order requiring one party to pay the other money. In courts of law, either side normally has the option of having a jury decide those aspects that have to do with finding the truth among disputed facts.

Courts of equity: In general, courts of equity make decisions that usually order a party do something other than simply pay money. In courts of equity, judges make all the decisions. Juries are almost never involved. But in all courts, judges, not juries, decide all disputes about the rules or the law.

Remedies: What the plaintiff is requesting from the court.

Injunction: A remedy in which a court orders some action other than paying money. A mandatory injunction is a type of injunction where a party is ordered to take an action, as opposed to being restricted from an activity. Ordering a party not to compete because of a noncompete agreement is an injunction. But requiring them to return to their former employer all copies of that employer's customer list is a mandatory injunction.

Judgment: A court order that requires one party to pay money to the other.

Specific performance: A remedy in which a court order enforces that a party take an action required by a contract. Imagine for a moment that you have a contract with someone to purchase an apartment building. Between the time you sign the contract and the time of the closing, the building has gone up in value and the seller no longer wants to sell to you. Rather, the seller wants to sell to someone else who is offering more money. Under those circumstances, you can probably get an order for specific performance where the judge requires the building owner to sign a deed that conveys it to you as specified in the contract.

Issues of fact: Although trials usually involve many arguments about the law, such as whether certain evidence is admissible, the ultimate purpose of a trial is to determine the issues of fact—simply, questions of who really said what to whom, whether the goods that a company delivered were in conformance with the purchase order specifications, or whether the defendant really signed the contract (as opposed to the plaintiff having forged his signature).

Motion to dismiss: A motion asking that a complaint be dismissed because what it alleges is insufficient to entitle the plaintiff to relief. This type of motion is presented without any evidence and is decided simply by what the complaint does or does not say. (Lawyers like to say that this is decided "on the face" of the complaint.) A motion to dismiss assumes that all allegations of *facts* in the complaint are true, but asks the judge to dismiss the complaint because even after accepting that these allegations are true, the plaintiff would still not be entitled to recovery. In other words, to win a motion to dismiss, the defendant must persuade the judge that the complaint does not state a cause of action.

Motion for summary judgment: A motion in which the judge is told that because of matters in addition to those addressed in the complaint (such as deposition testimony, affidavits, or documents), there are no disputes about material facts and that, based on the undisputed facts, the moving party is entitled to win without a trial.

Pretrial conference: Simply a conference among the parties and the judge before the trial. Almost all judges have pretrial conferences, which can serve many purposes. Some feel that their job is simply to decide those questions brought before their court. They believe that they can best help people settle cases if they simply move those cases along as quickly as possible. That way, the parties will be forced to decide early on whether they will settle or face the risks and expenses of a trial. These judges view pretrial conferences as a means of reviewing the trial plans of the lawyers and resolving as many legal disputes as possible so that the trial can proceed quickly. Often, all evidentiary exhibits are marked and objections are decided in advance.

However, many other judges, knowing how people often find it hard to compromise, will ask, or insist, that the parties appear in the judge's chambers for a pretrial conference focused on trying to help them reach a settlement. In these situations, the judge will usually act in a manner similar to that of a mediator. As you can imagine, an articulate, smart, and forceful judge, with many years of prior experience as a trial lawyer, can, while still being fair to both sides, be very effective and persuasive in bringing about a settlement. It is not uncommon for a client to get right up to the eve of trial and not understand the risks of losing. This is not always the lawyer's fault. Many clients have been told about these risks and simply chose to ignore them. However, it is hard to continue to ignore those risks after being told of them while meeting alone with the judge.

Discovery: This is the procedure available to both parties to find out about (discover) the facts that the other party knows or will try to prove in at trial. Discovery was designed so that trials, in theory, will more accurately uncover the truth and the outcome will depend less upon cleverly hiding evidence until it is brought out to surprise the other side. In practice, discovery can have many strategic goals other than just trying to see the other side's cards and hoping that they will not ask to see yours. For example, through discovery, you can educate the other side about weaknesses in their case that they have ignored. Or, you can make sure that they know that you know about their weaknesses. Also, by making the other side spend a great deal of money on attorney's fees during discovery, you can dramatically change their risk/benefit analysis. The scope of permissible discovery is generally very broad, with each side being entitled to discover all information (memories, testimony, computer records, emails or computer copies of emails, or documents) that is either relevant or likely to lead to relevant information. Discovery is generally done through four methods:

Depositions: A meeting where one person (the witness or *deponent*) is required to answer, under oath and before a court reporter (but not a judge), questions asked by a lawyer concerning any matter deemed likely to lead to relevant information. Virtually anyone can be deposed. Depositions rarely are evidence that can be used at the trial. But deposition testimony still has many other valuable uses. It can be used to support or defeat a motion for summary judgment. It is a very effective way to evaluate what a prospective witness will say at the trial, figure out how to rebut this testimony, determine how to best cross-examine that witness at the trial, and evaluate how persuasive the judge or jury is likely to find that witness. Also, once people have testified at a deposition, their testimony is preserved, which can prevent that witness from later changing testimony at trial. Pointing out that a witness should not be believed because he changed testimony is called *impeaching* the witness based on prior inconsistent statements.

Interrogatories: These are written questions posed by one party that the other party is required to answer.

Requests for admissions: These are written requests by one party that require the other party to either admit or deny specific statements of fact. Requests to admit can be used for various purposes: to limit the need to take depositions, to educate the other side as to the weaknesses of its case, or to avoid having to prove facts that the other side knows are true.

Document discovery/requests to produce: In litigation, each side is entitled, by serving requests to produce, to obtain copies of all the discoverable documents—i.e., those that are relevant or likely to lead to relevant information.

Trial: The event where a judge or a jury hears evidence and then resolves disputed facts by deciding the truth—that is, by deciding what happened. At a trial, the parties take turns presenting evidence. The plaintiff goes first, and when the plaintiff has finished, the defendant gets a turn. The plaintiff is then given a chance to rebut the defendant's evidence, and at times the defendant is given another chance as well. In business trials, each side has the chance to insist on a jury. This must be done very early in the case. When a jury is involved, it must first decide the facts from the evidence presented and then determine the outcome by applying the law to these facts. The job of the judge is to apply the law in conducting the trial and then instruct the jury in how the law is applicable to this case.

Bench trial: A trial where there is no jury and the judge determines both the law and the facts. Bench trials are usually shorter and less expensive since a great deal of a lawyer's time in preparing for trial involves work done to prepare for choosing jurors, presenting information to them, and writing the instructions which they want the judge to eventually give to the jury. Also, at a bench trial the rules of evidence are relaxed because it is believed that the judge, unlike a jury, can hear irrelevant evidence and know what to ignore.

Pretrial order: A requirement by many judges that, before a case goes to trial, the lawyers get together to agree on a statement of the uncontested facts, the contested facts, and the contested issues of law. It's often required that the parties state who will testify and what documents will be introduced into evidence. This causes the lawyers to focus on their cases and identify and understand the contested issues that the trial will need to resolve. It also saves judges a great deal of time by allowing them to prepare in advance for the rulings that will be required on evidence and law. The process of complying with a pretrial order is usually very time consuming and, since lawyers normally charge by the hour, very expensive.

Motions in liminae: A request to a judge made shortly before the trial for a ruling on a specific evidentiary problem. For example, in a case involving the question of why a machine malfunctioned, the plaintiff may know that the defendant plans to call as its expert a man who serviced and repaired machines of this type for thirty years. The plaintiff could present a motion in limini to bar this person's testimony on the grounds that he is not an expert since he does not have an advanced degree in mechanical engineering.

Evidence: Not everything is evidence. The rules of evidence are very complicated and it is often unclear what a judge will do when asked to rule on a critical piece of evidence. Knowing in advance of the trial how the judge will rule on such a question can be very helpful in evaluating the strength of your case, creating a strategy for dealing with an adverse ruling, and determining whether to settle. During a trial the judge or jury is allowed to hear only information that is reliable and has a rational bearing on the truth. Witnesses are expected to testify as to what they saw, felt, smelled, or heard; their nonexpert opinions of why someone did something or whether someone was telling the truth are of minimal value as testimony. For example, many people are convinced that they can tell whether someone is telling the truth by looking into their eyes when they are speaking. However, their opinion of a witness's truthfulness would not be allowed in court as evidence. People who are genuine "experts" may testify as to their opinions. For instance, consider a trial intended to determine who was responsible for an automobile accident. The driver said that he lost control while driving safely and claims that the accident occurred when the wheel broke off of the axle because it was improperly attached. The defendant says that although the wheel is now broken off, it broke because of the impact of the accident and not before the accident. Since only experts are allowed to give opinions, there is considerable debate as to who qualifies as an expert. Often both sides have equally qualified experts who have diametrically opposed opinions. Many feel that the rules of evidence applied at a trial are unnecessarily complicated and exclude too much useful information. This is the subject of considerable debate within the legal community, especially about who may testify as an expert. Notably, in arbitrations and in bench trials, the rules of evidence are normally much more relaxed.

Hearsay: A type of unreliable evidence. Since a trial is to determine the truth based on reliable evidence, certain types of potential evidence are excluded because they are uniquely unreliable. Hearsay is (a) an out-of-court statement, (b) made by someone other than the witness, that (c) is being testified to in order to prove the truth of what was said. For example, a witness in a dispute regarding whether one company owed money to the other would not be allowed to testify that he was told by the accounts payable clerk that the money was actually due. That would be hearsay. To get this testimony heard at the trial, the accounts payable clerk would have to be called as a witness. For better or worse, there are many exceptions to the hearsay rule. All these exceptions have to do with circumstances where the testimony may be hearsay, but nevertheless has a high likelihood of being reliable. For example, imagine a murder victim who, just prior to dying, says to a police officer, "My brother shot me." The police officer is called to testify as to what the victim said, and the defendant's lawyer objects because this is "classic" hearsay. The prosecutor will remind the judge that there is an exception to the hearsay rule for "dying declarations" since it is believed that people who know they are about to die are uniquely motivated to tell the truth. Another exception is for declarations made to a priest during confession.

Direct vs. circumstantial evidence: Direct evidence is what a witness directly experiences through her own senses. Circumstantial evidence is what the witness assumed happened under circumstances where the assumption is almost assuredly correct. A classic example of circumstantial evidence is when someone wakes up and sees snow on the ground, thus believing that it had snowed that night. Since the person had been sleeping, he did not know if it snowed, and so he assumed it had because there was no other logical explanation for the snow on the ground. It is not logical, for example, to think that someone had brought it from another town and sprinkled on his lawn.

Prima facie case: At a trial, the plaintiff is required to present a "prima facie" case. This means that the plaintiff must present enough evidence during their turn to win—to prove all the elements of the plaintiff's case.

Jury instructions: A lecture the judge gives the jury telling them what law should be applied to the facts that the jury is to determine. Jury instructions are normally not finalized until just before the trial is underway. Often, the judge decides critical questions of law in finalizing the jury instructions, and the judge's resolution of these questions can materially shape the outcome of the trial. A simple example is the judge's determination of the standard of proof. In other words, we all know that in criminal trials, the prosecution must prove the defendant's guilt "beyond a reasonable doubt." But in business trials the judge will instruct the jury that they must decide disputed facts based on the "weight of the evidence," which means that a fact is more likely true than not. However, in some cases, critical facts must be proven by the "preponderance of the evidence," which is a higher standard.

Motion for directed verdict: A motion made by the defendant, after the plaintiff has rested, which says that the defendant should not have to proceed any further, for one of two reasons. Either the plaintiff did not introduce any evidence regarding a critical fact or did not present a prima facial case (for example, although there was evidence presented that the plaintiff's car was hit by the defendant's car, there was no evidence of the plaintiff being injured), or because there is no way that the jury could have believed the plaintiff's evidence on a critical fact (for example, although there was clear evidence of the plaintiff's having been *treated* for a broken arm three days after the accident, the testimony was equally clear that on *the day after* the accident, the plaintiff was seen playing baseball with no pain, and thus the plaintiff's arm must have been broken at some point after the accident). Under these circumstances, the judge could rule that no rational jury could rule for the plaintiff, and thus the defendant should not have to proceed with its defense.

Motion to reconsider: A motion asking the trial judge to reconsider a ruling. Judges, like all human beings, make mistakes. Good judges will admit when this occurs and correct their mistake. For example, at a trial the judge might rule that the plaintiff could not present the testimony of a witness who the plaintiff had offered as an expert. After the trial, the plaintiff's lawyer is able to find prior cases where the state's supreme court had ruled that witnesses with these qualifications could testify as experts, and that barring this person's testimony is the type of error that would result in a reversal on appeal. Under these circumstances, the trial judge might reconsider that ruling and order a new trial.

Motion for judgment notwithstanding the verdict (NOV): A request for the judge to overrule a jury because the jury's verdict is so far-fetched that it has to have been motivated by bias or undue sympathy. Often, once a jury is organized and has sat through the trial, a judge will let it reach a decision, even if the judge thinks that the case can be decided only one way. The judge hopes that the jury will reach what the judge thinks is the appropriate conclusion. But there are times when the judge might reflect for a day or so on the evidence and then decide that the jury had simply reached an emotional, and not a rational, conclusion. For example, imagine a trial at which a once-beautiful young woman has been terribly disfigured by using a face cream that had been incorrectly manufactured. Since the company that manufactured the face cream has no insurance and is bankrupt, the woman has sued the drugstore at which she claims the face cream was purchased. Even though there is almost no proof that the face cream she used had been purchased from the defendant drugstore, a jury might, out of undue sympathy, award a judgment against that defendant so that the woman might have the money to pay for plastic surgery. Under these circumstances, the judge might enter a judgment NOV, concluding that no reasonable jury could ever reach the conclusion that the contaminated face cream had been purchased from the defendant.

Motion for a new trial: Simply a motion asking for a new trial. Succeeding on this type of motion would require persuading the judge that new evidence was found that could not have been known previously, or that the judge made mistakes at the trial that would have led to a different decision by the jury. Not all mistakes or new evidence will lead to a new trial.

Review by an appellate court: As one would imagine, judges are very unlikely to reverse their own decisions or the decisions of juries after a trial. Trial judges, who are decisive by profession, often feel that once a matter is decided they should move on to the next case. Many lawyers feel it is a waste of time to even approach the trial judge to correct an error. In these situations, the option is to present the problem to an appellate court.

Appeal: A request to a higher court to overturn or reverse the ruling of the trial judge or the verdict of the jury. There is almost always the opportunity to present an appellate court with a claim that the proceedings before a trial judge were done incorrectly. Appellate courts are usually made up of three judges whose job it is to hear appeals. The United States Supreme Court is made up of nine judges. State supreme courts have nine or seven judges. Some people mistakenly think that the appellate process provides a new trial to anyone unhappy with how their trial turned out. This is simply not true. There are two very critical limits to the appellate process.

First, a person involved in a lawsuit can rarely appeal until the trial is over. In other words, even though the judge may make a ruling early in the case that you think is wrong and will severely limit your chances of winning, you almost always have to finish the trial before you can get an appellate court to hear your arguments about this mistake. Second, an appeal is *not* a new trial! The goal of a trial is to determine the facts in a setting that is fair to both sides. The goal of an appeal is *not* to determine whether the trial reached the "correct" result. Rather, it is to determine whether the *process* the trial followed was fair and whether the law was correctly applied to the facts determined by the judge or jury.

Thus, during an appeal, the trial judge's rulings as to law will be evaluated on the basis of whether those rulings denied someone a fair trial or whether those rulings were right or wrong. This standard is called a *de novo review*. For example, granting a motion to dismiss or motion for summary judgment is a ruling of law about which the appellate court will conduct a *de novo* review.

However, the appellate court will not determine whether the facts as decided by the jury were right or wrong. Appellate courts are mindful that the trial judge had the unique opportunity to see the witnesses, to hear their responses, to see their demeanors; appellate courts assume that trial courts are the best setting to determine those facts. On the other hand, it is possible that mistakes can be made through prejudice or emotion. Thus, when determining what to do about how a trial determined the facts of a case, the appellate court applies a much higher standard of review: whether it was "clearly erroneous" or "against the manifest weight of the evidence." For example, imagine that the defendant in an automobile accident case argues that the plaintiff was drunk and careless. If the trial's jury decided that the plaintiff was sober, this "factual" conclusion would not be reversed on appeal unless the appellate court, after reading the transcript of the trial, was convinced that it was against the manifest weight of the evidence.

The legal system is designed so that all people get their "day in court"—a trial that gives them a fair chance. But this means that the rules are structured so that unhappy litigants don't get what some lawyers call "two bites at the apple." People are entitled to one trial. Mistakes might be made, but not all mistakes mean that there should be a new trial. It is obviously a shame when the trial goes poorly, a lawyer makes a mistake, a witness gets nervous and makes a slip of the tongue, or a party loses a critical piece of evidence. But the system is structured to give people a fair trial—not a perfect trial or a trial that protects them from their own bad judgment.

Notice of appeal: The document that starts an appeal. It is a notice to the other side, the judge, and the appellate court that you plan to appeal. The rules regarding an appeal usually require that this notice be prepared and filed within thirty days of the trial court's final judgment.

Record on appeal: The written transcript of the proceedings—everything that was said and all documents that were presented—before the trial court. Evidence or testimony that was not presented to the trial court can almost never be presented to an appellate court since it is the appellate court's job to consider only whether the trial was fair based on what was presented at that time.

Appellate briefs: These are the written papers the parties submit to the appellate court once the record on appeal has been filed. The party that loses before the trial court is normally called the *appellant*. Appellants always file their briefs first. The party that wins in the trial court is called the *appellee,* and files a brief that replies to the appellant's brief. The appellant then has the chance to file a brief that responds to the reply brief.

Appellate argument: These oral arguments take place after all preliminary documents have been filed and examined by the judges. This is an opportunity for the parties' lawyers to speak to the panel of judges. No witnesses are heard and no new testimony or evidence is presented. Often, the judge will ask the lawyers questions to probe how a lawyer's position will affect future cases, whether the lawyer's position is consistent with past cases, and the potential impact the lawyer's position will have on commerce or the judicial system. After the appellate argument, the appellate judges normally take weeks (or even months) during which they write a decision—the *opinion*—that explains their ruling and their reasoning.

Appeal to the Supreme Court: A case can almost never be appealed directly to the Supreme Court of the United States, or the supreme court of a state. Rather, each of these courts has its own rules as to which types of cases it will hear. Normally, for a business case to be heard by a supreme court, that court must be persuaded that your case is of sufficient importance to the judicial system to justify taking time to hear it. Usually, supreme courts agree to hear cases that raise questions of law that fall into one of two categories: first, questions of law the resolution of which will affect many other cases; and second, questions of law that have been decided in different ways by various appellate courts, for which resolutions of these differences would be helpful to many other cases.

Writ of certiorari: A request to a supreme court that it hear an appeal from a lower appellate court, also known as a "petition for leave to appeal." In order to have one of those courts hear the appeal, the judges must be satisfied that it presents a unique question of law that is of importance to the entire judicial system.

Enforcement of a Judgment or Other Court Order

Many business owners are surprised when they discover, after they've won a trial, that the court order which they spent so much time, anxiety, and money to obtain is merely a piece of paper with a judge's signature. You cannot cash it in at a bank, nor will the defendant always simply hand you a check. One of the critical decisions our country's founders made was to abolish the debtors prisons that existed in England. This historical fact has profound ramifications for court orders. Every day, hundreds of people are shocked and disappointed to find that someone's failure to pay money pursuant to a court order, even after tens of thousands of dollars were invested in legal fees to get a judge to determine that that money was due, will not result in jail.

The winner of a judgment often becomes merely the proud new owner of a court order and must figure out what to do to turn that piece of paper into money. There are various methods for turning court orders into cash. These are referred to as *post-judgment proceedings.*

Citation to discover assets: A court order procured by the person to whom the money is owed (the judgment creditor) that compels the person who owes the money (the judgment debtor), or any third party, to appear in court or a lawyer's office to answer questions under oath or produce documents that will help uncover the debtor's assets. Once she finds these assets, the judgment creditor can have the sheriff *garnish* these assets to satisfy the judgment. A citation can also prohibit transfers of that property. Although you can't go to jail for not paying the debt, you can go to jail if you are found in contempt of court for not obeying a citation to discover assets.

Fraudulent conveyances: Illegal practices used by some judgment debtors to avoid paying debts by transferring their assets to a family member or trusted friend, and then getting it back after the judgment creditor gives up on collecting the payment. The legal system has been dealing with this problem for many years.

Garnishment: A process that allows a judgment creditor to obtain a court order requiring a third party to deliver money or property owed to a judgment debtor. The fact that a judgment debtor has property that is being held by someone else does not prevent it from being taken to satisfy a judgment. For instance, a judgment creditor can garnish a judgment debtor's bank account. Or, if a judgment debtor owns an apartment building, the judgment creditor may garnish the rents that are due from the tenants, thereby requiring the tenants to pay rent directly to the judgment creditor.

Judgment liens: The right to take and hold or sell the property of a judgment debtor as a payment. Just like your mortgage is a lien on your house that entitles your mortgage lender to be paid before other creditors when your house is sold, so, too, can a judgment be a lien on a person's property. This judgment lien can be foreclosed the same way a mortgage is foreclosed—that is, by a sale of the property with the proceeds going to pay the judgment creditor. So, if a person's wealth consists only of an apartment building, a judgment against that person can become a lien on that building that can result in it being sold to pay the judgment.

Execution: When a sheriff physically and, if necessary, forcefully takes from the judgment debtor property that can be sold to satisfy the judgment. Lawyers often talk about "executing" on a judgment. This has nothing to do with anyone being killed. But the sheriff might literally go to debtors' houses to take their furniture, TV, and fancy stereo equipment to raise money to pay off their judgments.

Contempt of court: A charge made by a judge against a party for having disobeyed a court order. This charge can be vital to the enforcement of judgments, particularly those that involve injunctions. For instance, if someone is ordered not to compete with their former partner in a business and they proceed to do so, he runs the risk of being held in contempt by the judge and being arrested.

Attachment: A unique type of court process in which a person can take possession of property owned by the defendant *before* the trial and *before* a judgment has been entered. Normally, a person cannot take the property of another until after the trial, but in almost every state, there is a statute that specifies when an attachment can issue. With an attachment, however, the plaintiff must put up a bond to guarantee that the defendant will be paid damages if it turns out that the defendant does not owe the plaintiff any money (and thus the property has been taken improperly). If the plaintiff ends up getting a judgment, the property that was attached can be sold to satisfy the judgment.

About the Author

HENRY C. KRASNOW, JD, is an attorney who has worked with small and mid-sized businesses, among other clients, for almost forty years. He is senior partner at the Chicago-based business law firm Krasnow Saunders Cornblath, LLP. He can be contacted at hkrasnow@ksc-law.com or through www.ksc-law.com.